WOOF NOTES

Life with Dogs, Volume One
Jacque Stonehocker

Well-Inspired Ink

About Well-Inspired Ink
The Love Story That Started It All

Well-Inspired Ink ©

There's a well outside a small town nestled in the foothills of the San Juan mountains, dug deep, tapping into the clear mountain water of the Western Slope of Colorado. The well sits between two homesteads, one on the hill and one in the valley.

A lovely, tender-hearted teenage girl, the oldest of her siblings, and a poet at heart, had the chore of going to the well to draw water for the family. A quiet, thoughtful, teenage boy lived in the home on the hill.

One day, he spotted her, and decided to get some water from the well *right then* too. It was love at first sight. Frequent trips to the well were no longer a chore. Leonard and Eula Mae met there as often as possible. It was the beginning of their lifelong love story.

They raised a family together through the hard challenges brought about by the Great Depression, then World War II. He served in the Army in the Philippines while she cared for their three children at home.

When the war ended and he returned home, he worked for the Civil Conservation Corps (CCC) in Colorado before they moved to Utah for a job with the railroad out of dire necessity. They had another daughter, my mom.

Somehow they managed to raise four children during those extremely difficult times, and they raised them with so much love, laughter, and a strong moral compass. I am filled with gratitude for the lessons of empathy, a solid work ethic, determination, kindness, spirituality, love and humor they instilled in me. They didn't have a life full of worldly riches, but they lived a very rich life.

Grandma & Grandpa were both creatives. He could figure out and fix or build just about anything. She wrote poetry, crocheted, canned, gardened and loved photography. They loved the mountains and appreciated the beauty in nature. They valued books, often ordering them and paying for a series in installments. I inherited my love of nature and books from them and from my mom.

My creative journey began at that well. Without their love, their relationship, and the many ways they showed their creative genius in everyday ways, I would not be the writer that I am.

May you be inspired to nourish and share *your* creativity too. They would've loved that.

Thank you for reading this Well-Inspired Ink title.

Dedication

To each of the dogs. Especially the "hard" dogs. I am a better, more empathetic, human because of you.

Kenai

Introduction

"We're not, after all, separate from the animal kingdom. We're part of it." ~ Jane Goodall

empathy

[em-puh-thee]

1. The ability [and desire] to understand another sentient being's feelings

2. To place one's steps in the footsteps, or paw prints, of another

3. To care as deeply for another as we care for ourselves, maybe more.

My prayer, my longing, is that the articles, essays and stories shared in WOOF NOTES: Life with Dogs, Volume One will raise our consciousness, open our hearts, increase our empathy toward our companion animals, and each other.

Preface

This book began over a decade ago, though I didn't know it at the time. I responded to a contest call for pictures of dogs wearing something green.

I submitted a photo of our Rottweiler, Sadie, wearing a bright green backpack. Her Rotti head was posed in a tilt, ears perked up, smile on her face and a mischievous twinkle in her eyes. I emailed my submission.

And gained an amazing human friend.

Dixie Dahle-Loosli, the editor, wrote back to say that she sensed I was a writer.

I was stunned that she could discern that from an email. She didn't know about my long-held dream to become an author.

WOOF NOTES: Life with Dogs, Volume One is a collection of previously published fiction and non-fiction pieces I've written for The Animal Companion Magazine since 2013. Each piece can be read in its original form at https://myanimalcompanion.com/ and at https://thecompanionanimalmagazine.blogspot.com/

Dixie has guided my journey with generosity and kindness. Her editorial eye is keen and I'm grateful for all that she continues to teach me.

Each piece has deepened my understanding, about the special relationships we share with our companion animals, about myself, and about writing.

I have a decal on my car that says, "Dogs are proof God loves us." I feel that love, and I am grateful.

My Car Decal

Contents

Essays & Nonfiction

Sadie & Lexi Sporting Their Life Jackets and Doggles©

Companion Animals: An Integral Part of Our Lives

The companion animals we share our lives with are so much more than pets. They are family members.

As we go through our hectic days, they wait in hopeful expectation for our presence, our touch, our smiles, and our delight in their company. By our sides and in our hearts, their presence enriches our lives beyond measure.

We need and rely on them, and they need and rely on us. Just by being themselves, they become an integral part of our lives.

Our companion animals greet us eagerly, whether we have been away for five hours or five minutes. They give us their *whole* hearts. Their love for us is honest and pure. We are the place they want to be.

It is an honor to have our companions, our helpers, our protectors, and our hilarious tricksters by our sides.

Snuggling with them is medicine for the soul. They are unmatched treasures.

Life has taught me that the right dog will be sent to my side at just the right time – even if I think I'm not ready.

Each new partner has important things to teach us through their lens of unconditional love. Our companion animals only want one thing: an ever-closer heart-connection with us.

The world is a complicated blur. In the midst of that chaos and stress, we have a refuge. With our steadfast companion animals in our homes, and by our sides, we can share comfort, enjoy an oasis of peace, and focus on living a life filled with unconditional love.

We can give our best to them by being *truly* present and living in the moment *with* them.

Their lives are so brief. There are never enough days together. When they leave our side, to go their rest, there's an empty spot that no other can fill.

However, we can honor their memory in a beautiful way – by adopting another.

Our lives are best lived with our companion animals just a scritch, a scratch, a belly-rub, a tug toy, or a game of fetch away.

Pearlie, Modeling Her Coat
While At Play©

A Lifetime Commitment

Sassy: A Smart, Chatty Girl © Cathy Smihula

A post circulated on social media recently. It was a photo of a dog and his human that had been taken many years ago, when the dog was a young puppy. Next to that was a current photo of the two.

In the current photo, both sported some grey hair, and the same happy expressions.

I was touched at what was so clearly illustrated. The man in that photo was, and still is, committed to keeping and cherishing his dog for the duration.

A *lifetime* commitment.

Bringing a pet, an animal companion, into your life and home is a *lifetime* commitment.

Animal shelters are overflowing with companion animals who have been picked up as strays, or surrendered by the families that they were devoted to and loved with their whole hearts.

I am certain that most of those dumped dogs would wag, dance, and kiss those deserters if they walked back into the shelter days or weeks later. Dogs love their people.

A dog's devotion never dies. The human heart, however, is fickle and can be so brutal.

Can you imagine devoting your life and love to a family for years, only to have them drop you off at a shelter because you are old, or sick, and need more care than you once did? Can you imagine the pain of that separation? Can you imagine the fear and anxiety if ill, blind, or deaf, or all three? Can you imagine being abandoned by your humans when you need them *most*?

Can you imagine the upset, confusion, and fear of a dog as their "family" dumps them at a shelter, signs a paper, then walks out and drives away - *without them*?! They likely left the house together, the dog thinking they were going on a fun adventure! Only to be left scared and bewildered, waiting for their "humans" to return for them.

The best part of the day for a dog is *any* part that they get to spend in cherished moments of play and interaction with their humans. Dogs wait for their humans to return home and find it well worth the wait. They do their best to manage their emotions until we return.

Maybe the anxiety gets a little too intense one day, it gets a bit out-of-paw, and a roll of toilet paper gets shredded, or some socks get stolen and chewed. Is it really fair for a devoted dog to end up in a shelter, abandoned by the humans they love, facing all of the noise, fear, amped up collective anxiety, and the possibility of being killed for that? NO!

There are compassionate, wise, and affordable solutions: a dog walker, doggy daycare, or going home at lunch time to take your dog out to relieve themselves and have a moment of connection together. You will *both* benefit.

Some claim they don't have enough time for their dogs. I wonder - why did they get a dog then?

This is a common reason given for surrender when a dog is in their adolescence. The dog brain does not mature until they are 2-3 years old. Their bodies mature faster than their brains do. Is that a fair reason to abandon them? NO!

Begin training when you first bring them into your lives. Positive, fair, balanced and rewarding training is the antidote. Dogs need a job and an outlet. If their needs are satisfied, they will be calmer, less destructive, and less anxious.

It is *our* job to meet their needs.

Bringing a pet, an animal companion, into your life and home is a *lifetime* commitment.

That commitment does not last only until an inconvenience occurs. They are family.

They are the most devoted companions many will *ever* have, given the chance. They love their humans unconditionally. They hold nothing back. They trust us.

If we allow them to, they will commit their entire lives to us, from our first meeting, until their final breath.

Don't we owe them the same?

Conquering Post-Adoption Challenges

Pearlie©

Adopting a new companion animal into your family can be a wonderful experience and it can be a challenge.

By the time your new furry family member arrives in their forever home, he or she may have endured trials and life challenges that you, as the new and hopefully forever parent, can not imagine:

abuse, both physical and mental, lack of proper nutrition, and medical neglect.

These dog-kids sometimes enter your home unscathed. Others experience confusion, abandonment, visceral fear, and utter grief and loneliness.

It is now your challenge and responsibility to help them heal from any residual issues your new family member may have.

Perhaps they've lost their home, neighborhood, animal friends, and entire human community due to the death of their person, or fought to survive as a stray where every moment held potential danger and lacked any certainty of a next meal or clean drink of water.

Maybe their former "family" decided they were too old and dumped them off at a shelter, or on a roadside, only to replace them with a new puppy for Christmas. Perhaps their only sin was being an adolescent who needed training, patience, and compassion.

IMPORTANT FACT

Dogs' brains do not fully develop until they are 2-3 years old, just as the human brain doesn't fully develop until we are in our twenties or beyond. Their bodies may appear mature long before their brains mature. Just like humans.

SHELTER DOGS

Many dogs do not fare well in shelters. Confined to small spaces in a noisy environment where all of their canine companions feel anxious and uncertain, we can only imagine how fearful they must be.

DOGS, THE ULTIMATE OPTIMISTS

Dogs thrive when they have security, a job, and an outlet. Dogs are optimists. When their big day arrives with the possibility that they are leaving the shelter, their hearts leap with joy. Chosen by a human, their emotions soar.

DOGS NEED TO PLEASE THEIR HUMANS

The entire experience, from abandonment to acceptance and finally, adoption, is an incredible amount of change for a dog to process. Dogs live in the moment. They are so adaptable. However, due to the trauma and instability of their pre-adoption lives, they may display unwanted behaviors.

REAL LIFE IN A REAL HOME

Once living in a new environment, your dog may regress in potty-training, become destructive, withdraw emotionally into their private world, refuse food, and exhibit other behaviors as they decompress.

DO NOT TAKE IT PERSONALLY and DO NOT PUNISH THEM!

Take a deep breath. Remind yourself of the lifelong commitment you've made to help this precious, sentient being.

Dogs ask for so little, yet give humans their all.

At first, everything in your new dog's new home equals uncertainty. Our job is to have patience, empathy, and compassion.

THE 3 - 3 - 3 RULE

The 3-3-3 Rule explains what to expect and what to do, the first three days after your new dog comes home, how to manage the following three weeks, and how to follow up for the next three months.

NOTE: These guidelines are the *minimum*. Depending on your dog's personality, and past life, each time frame might take much longer. Your dog may need their own 8-8-8 Rule, or longer. Be patient. It will be worth it!

THE FIRST THREE DAYS

The first three days (minimum) are for decompressing. Your new family member needs time and a quiet comfortable space to rest. Do not force interaction; allow your new dog to come to you. This may be an overwhelming time. Expect your new dog to sleep, avoid interaction, or test boundaries.

SETTING BOUNDARIES

Your new dog may not understand boundaries. Set boundaries early, but give them space and compassion. Your new companion will still be learning boundaries by testing them. They are not trying to be naughty or cause you stress. They are simply trying to decide what is expected of them.

Begin a daily routine you can maintain long-term. Dogs like routine.

Dogs are sensitive, emotional beings. By the time your dog comes to his or her new home, they may have lost so much. Patience is key.

THE ESCAPE ARTIST

Your new dog may want to escape. Be vigilant, have a leash attached to a harness when you open doors. This is not a good time to have a doggy door accessible. Most dog rescue organizations and private parties as well, ask adopters to provide a secure, locked fence to ensure your new dog stays home.

MEDICAL/DIET

It is extremely important you make sure your new dog is vetted. That includes all immunizations, including Rabies (a Utah State law). Your new dog, especially a rescue dog, has likely been through many changes in diet. A soft, bland diet for the first few days may be helpful, especially if you notice anxiety.

Enrichment toys can help ease chewing and anxiety. Sniffing, chewing and licking are all calming behaviors. Be sure to use safe toys like Kong food puzzles, or licking mats.

Ask your veterinarian what would be safe and appropriate for your new dog. Never give them anything made of rawhide. Ever. The chemical processes used to make rawhide are toxic. Always supervise when giving your dog a new toy or chew.

Work closely with a Veterinarian to resolve any gastrointestinal issues.

HUMAN INTERACTIONS

Your new companion may be in survivor mode and feel the need to lash out. Keep people and other household pets at a distance. You can allow your dog a private area using gates, a circular playpen or a designated kennel.

Children may need to distance themselves for the first several weeks. ***Remember, the dog is not there to entertain the children.*** Set firm boundaries with children, and be sure to uphold them.

Never allow children to spend unsupervised time with the dog. Teach children to refrain from hugging, kissing, sitting on, poking, prodding, or hitting a dog. Teach them to never run up to the dog. The speed and motion may frighten an already unsure dog.

KIDS WILL BE KIDS

Teach children to always be kind to animals. Show them how to gently pet a dog. Help them to understand that unusual motions, such as reaching over a dog's head or neck, may be interpreted by the new dog as an aggressive or dominant action.

Children should never touch a dog's food or toys. These are precious items, especially to a rescued dog.

Children tend to be understandably excited and overstimulated regarding their new family pet. However, their increased energy and noise, combined with the dog's need to rest and decompress, can easily lead to a stressful situation that results in a bite.

BITES ARE PREDICTABLE & PREVENTABLE

A bite is 100% PREDICTABLE and PREVENTABLE. It is the humans' responsibility to ensure that children and dogs are not put in a compromising position. Discuss these boundaries with children before bringing your newly adopted dog home.

Choose prevention; it provides a better outcome.

THE FIRST THREE WEEKS

TIME TO TRAIN

During the next several weeks, your new dog should become more emotionally comfortable, and you will observe a more relaxed, happy, attentive affect in your dog's demeanor.

At this point, training in short sessions (5-10 minutes at first) is a good way to bond. Keep it fun and positive while giving praise and rewards.   Begin with basic obedience tasks. You may be surprised to observe your new companion is "trick-savvy"!

SAFEGUARDING YOUR NEW DOG

TOP PRIORITY in training is to work hard on developing a great recall. Your goal is to summon your dog and have them immediately return to you, no matter the situation, location, distractions, or environment.

Excellent recall saves dogs' lives. KEEP IT FUN! Use lots of praise when your dog comes to you. They'll be more likely to repeat the behavior.

Go on daily walks together. Be sure to use a collar that your dog cannot slip out of and get loose. You can use a harness with a safety tether that also attaches to the collar. That way, the dog will remain leashed and safe, even if they slip out of the collar.

SNIFFING

Allow your dog to sniff during appropriate breaks during walks. Sniffing is a powerful mental stimulation and is also calming to their nervous system. You will both benefit by allowing them to sniff.

TRAINERS & HUMAN TRAINING

It is crucial to work with a qualified professional trainer. You might search the directories of the Pet Professional Guild (https://www.petprofessionalguild.com/find-a-ppg-prof essional/), the Academy for Dog Trainers (https://academy fordogtrainers.com/trainers/), the Association for Professional Dog Trainers (https://training.apdt.com/?order=directory_c ompletion%20DESC&page=1), or the Certification Council for Professional Dog Trainers.

Do your due diligence by researching and reading reviews. Research the character, ethics, training methods, and business reputation of trainers you are considering. Attend and observe their training sessions to see first-hand which methods they teach.

Carefully select the kind of human you would trust a family member to, including who you would feel comfortable interacting with. Make sure the trainer is reputable. You are essentially placing the life and well-being of your new family member with a stranger. Choose carefully and logically.

Do not simply drop your dog off to be trained. You must be closely involved in in-person sessions.

Dog training is mostly human training.

Having expert help will make the transition so much better for you and your companion animal.

THE NEXT THREE MONTHS

YOUR DOG'S FAVORITE HUMAN

You are your dog's caretaker and most important person. Continue bonding, training, and exposing your dog to a vast array of new experiences. Life is now a grand adventure!

Keep life joyful. Hold firm boundaries. Make sure your new dog feels safe, secure, and assured of the behaviors you want. Keep it rewarding.

Dogs LOVE to work for a reward.

Always be mindful of their quirks and challenges. Their personalities are as individual as ours.

Keep them, and everyone else, safe by keeping them on-leash. This is a special time of building their confidence, and yours, as you strengthen your bond. They will continue to open up to you as their sense of security grows.

A FINAL WORD

Remember the commitment you made to them, and to yourself, to be their hero and their forever companion. It isn't their job to meet our needs. It is our job to meet *theirs*.

Every companion animal has tremendous gifts to give. Allow yourself the investment of time, education, patience, and compassionate work to build a stellar relationship with them.

The rewards far outweigh the challenges.

Canine Seat Belts Save Lives

Sleepy eyes light up, stubby-tails wag, making their whole bodies wiggle. Paws scramble across the floor in cartoon fashion. Dogs who, seconds ago, were fully engrossed in doggy dreams, spring to life with astonishing vigor.

No invitation needed. They know we are going for a car ride - an adventure! The sound of car keys, or the sight of us putting on our shoes, sends the whirlwind into motion.

We cannot open the car door fast enough for them.

Joy is infectious as they leap into the car, fling their noses out the open windows (never their whole heads, that is dangerous) and wait for the adventure to begin.

Oh, to live in the moment like dogs do!

The next task is to convince them to sit patiently in the back seat, for their protection and mine, while I buckle up their seat belts.

Safety first, right?

If I buckle myself in, but not my dogs, I am negligent in protecting my loving canine companions.

Auggie, Pearlie, and Aggie
Buckled In for a Car Ride©

DON'T LET THEM BECOME FUR MISSILES

Many pets do not recover after they are thrown from vehicles like missiles. Some may not die on impact, but become lost as they flee from the wreckage.

In shock, they only know that *you are gone.*

Perhaps they do not know where they are, or how to get home. Perhaps they are too injured to even try.

If human victims are rendered unconscious, first responders may not even *know* that dogs had been in the car.

SLIGHT SWERVE LEADS TO GRAVE INJURIES

Last summer, a local woman was driving to the dog park. Her well-behaved dog was relaxing in the back seat. She was always careful to keep the windows up far enough that he couldn't lean his shoulders out.

Without warning, the car in front of her stopped abruptly to avoid a head-on collision. She swerved, which sent her dog soaring out the small opening of the window.

In horror, she saw her loose, bloody dog yelping on the hot asphalt.

She later received a huge bill from the veterinarian hospital that she was not prepared for.

Her sweet boy recovered over the course of about three painful months. Many are not as fortunate.

LOOSE AND LOST

Many dogs become lost after an accident. A quick internet search reveals pages of headlines revealing the details of humans searching for their companion animals who were thrown from the crash site, or fled in panic.

A recent incident left the driver deceased and two dogs missing. The terrified pups fled the scene when first responders tried to help them.

The family, and the community, searched desperately for the dogs who were reported to be like the victim's children.

The driver would never have *intentionally* put them in harm's way.

Many days after the crash, a train operator reported seeing one of the dogs near the tracks - deceased. An expert pet tracker and the family were able to eventually find the other dog alive, injured, alone and traumatized.

STEPS WE CAN TAKE

What can we do to protect our beloved companion animals while traveling by car?

We began utilizing seat belts and harnesses with our dogs when we had two Rottweilers. One weighed about 95-pounds, and the other about 120-pounds. As we got in the car one day I thought about what could happen if I was in a wreck, or had to swerve, or make a quick stop to avoid one.

Our girls would be forced to tumble at a high rate of speed right over the top of me, likely injuring or killing us all.

I realized that there was no point in wearing my seatbelt, if I did not also secure our dogs.

I also knew that I could never bear the grief of losing them if I were the sole survivor of an accident.

BUCKLE THEM UP

What is the answer? An inexpensive seat belt and harness restraint system for dogs. Will canine seat belts save every dog in a crash? Sadly, no. Just as it is with humans.

We do know that survival rates are greatly increased when people wear seat belts. Study after study proves that theory. Laws are enacted in response.

Why not spend less than the cost of a fast-food meal to give our dogs a better chance at surviving a crash?

EASY FIXES

Canine safety has improved in the last decade. Some harnesses, seat belts and crates for dogs are now crash-tested. Utilizing equipment that has been crash-tested and found to improve safety is the best option.

If the expense of crash-tested equipment is prohibitive, the use of a good harness with a wide Y-strap to support the chest, with metal buckles and attachment points, plus a strong seatbelt strap with sturdy metal clasps, that has the ability to latch into the car's seatbelt device, or a child's car seat latch, is better than nothing.

If using the regular seat belt latch receptor, inexpensive adapters (called seat belt buckle guards) are available that cover the release button, so that your dog cannot free themselves (accidentally, or on purpose), by stepping on the release button.

CRATE CAUTION

Most crates that are for use at home simply crumple in a crash, putting our pets at additional risk of injury from the wire or plastic construction shattering and creating sharp pieces that could puncture your dog. If you'd prefer to use a crate for your pup, be sure to use one that is crash-tested.

Crash safety science has advanced tremendously in the past few decades; safer equipment is the result.

WE KNOW BETTER NOW

Growing up in the 70s, I rode in the back of open trucks, the back of station wagons, or in camper shells. Fun adventures for the time! Seat belts were not a consideration. Now, however, we would be horrified at the thought of allowing children to ride so unsafely.

Why would we put our beloved animal companions at risk?

Yet people do it all the time. I always wonder how much they do, or do *not*, love their animal companions. One brake tap can throw a dog through a window, or out of a truck bed, especially a flat bed.

NEVER LOOSE IN THE BACK OF AN SUV

The back compartment of an SUV is no match for a vehicle plowing into it due to a distracted driver. If there is a grate installed, it might keep the dog from flying into the front passenger compartment, but it won't do much to protect the dog. It will just be something painful for the dog to be slammed against with tremendous force. The injured pup will be crushed between the grate and the intruding vehicle or impaled on impact.

NEVER LET THEM RIDE UP FRONT – AIRBAG DANGERS

When we bought our Subaru, the owner of the dealership told me to *never* allow pets to ride in the front seat.

One reason is that pets are at increased risk of injury or death from the explosive force of the airbags, and from burns caused by the heat created by the rapid expansion of the gases that inflate them.

Just like small children, pets must *always* ride in the back seat. The risk of being injured or killed in a crash is exponentially higher in the front seat.

According to the NHTSA (National Highway Traffic Safety Administration, part of the U.S. Department of Transportation), "Buckling up helps keep you safe and secure inside your vehicle, whereas not buckling up can result in being totally ejected from the vehicle in a crash, which is almost always deadly…Air bags are not enough to protect you; in fact, the force of an air bag can seriously injure or even kill you if you're not buckled up."

HOW BAD DOES A CRASH NEED TO BE TO SET OFF AIR BAGS?

Frontal air bags are generally designed to deploy in moderate to severe frontal or near-frontal crashes, which are defined as crashes that are equivalent to hitting a solid, fixed barrier at 8 to 14 mph or higher. (This would be equivalent to striking a parked car of similar size at about 16 to 28 mph or higher). It does not take much to set off the airbags.

KEEP THEIR HEADS INSIDE THE CAR

Many dogs love nothing better than to stick their heads out the window, leaning their bodies out as far as they can. They love to sniff and take in all of the beautiful and exciting things around them.

This joyous habit can end in tragedy. Open windows are a big risk.

A dear friend, Jerrie Miller, told me a tragic story about a tremendously loved Great Pyrenees who was enjoying a ride with her head out the window.

A public transportation bus crossed into oncoming traffic, side-swiped their car and that gorgeous pup, decapitating her.

Everyone who witnessed, or heard about, her passing was traumatized, especially the students at the school where her hu-mom worked. The grief of losing her was unbearable.

Years later, the story of her ***avoidable*** accident, brings tears to the eyes of all who loved her.

Now that we know better, we *must do* better.

TRUE STORY

My former service dog, Pearlie, was always game for a car ride. She was also the most mellow, content dog while riding in the car.

If an unsuspecting person climbed into the front seat without knowing she was in the back seat - she was so silent that they might not know she was there.

Pearlie wasn't one to stick her head out the window, she merely rested a tiny bit of her velvety chin on the edge of the car, with the tip of her nose just barely sticking out into the breeze.

Thankfully, I had been in the habit of putting *every* dog riding with us in a harness and seatbelt for many years.

Our seatbelt habit paid off in a critical moment in the fall of 2013.

My husband and I noticed a home for sale in an area we'd dreamed of. It was near the golf course that we loved, and where we had learned to play. We weren't looking to move when we found it, but it seemed like a good fit for us.

We put our home on the market. Soon there were showings being scheduled. Each time our home was shown, I would pack up Pearlie, her dishes, and her toys, and go for a little drive.

Even though many of those appointments were last minute, sometimes without warning, I made sure that the two of us put on our seat belts for our short adventure.

Thank God.

We were driving on a familiar road, traveling slowly, about to make a right-hand turn, when Pearlie's clunky plastic dish stand and stainless steel dishes shifted, loudly clunking and clanging. The noise startled her and she jumped out of the window!

I pulled over, stopped, flung my door open, and frantically looked for Pearlie. Other cars were making the same turn, honking and swerving around us.

My heart prayed that Pearlie was safe, that her harness and seat-belt were still attached, that she wasn't injured, or running loose and terrified.

Tears welled in my eyes when I saw her.

She was casually hanging by her harness, completely still, tucked close against our car. She wasn't afraid.

Pearlie looked at me in her quiet way with an almost amused expression like, "Hey, Thumbs, I could use a little help here, please."

God answered the prayer that I didn't even have time to formulate or utter.

Pearlie and I had a challenging task–to get her back into the car. Her 85 pound body had the seatbelt pulled too tight to be able to unbuckle it. She was in a helpless position, hanging snugly against the outside of the car door. Her weight was almost more than I could lift. She did her part by being calm and still until I could lift her enough that she could get her front paws on the window frame. Pearlie used her strength to help lift the front end of her body, and I hefted her hind end through the window, making sure she had a safe landing on the seat.

Mission accomplished.

I moved her dishes to the floor up front, and wedged them in tight, so that they wouldn't move or make noise again.

Pearlie settled right in, she calmly rested her chin on the door, and resumed sniffing out the window.

Other drivers stopped to tell me they saw her fly out the window. They were afraid that *they* might be the ones to hit her. And they were each prepared to help me catch her if she was loose.

I am so grateful for their kindness.

They were as relieved as Pearlie and I that she was wearing her seatbelt and harness.

Pearlie's inexpensive harness, seat belt strap, and buckle cover saved her life and saved me a devastating grief that I would not have recovered from. The 20 seconds it took to buckle her in, and the $40.00 spent on the equipment, was time and money well-spent.

The whole incident with Pearlie solidified the continued use of seat belts for our animal companions, and of having them *always* ride in the back seat.

NEVER LET THEM RIDE ON YOUR LAP

Another huge risk for humans and pets, is having pets ride on laps, especially the driver's.

Children, and dogs, don't stand a chance if they are sitting on someone's lap, or hanging out of the window.

A distance of 10 inches needs to be maintained between the driver and the steering wheel, or the passenger and the dashboard.

It is impossible with a dog on your lap to keep the dog at ANY safe distance from the air bag or steering wheel. **Your body will *crush* them *into* the steering wheel**, if they are not ejected.

It's awful to imagine, but it is reality.

THE STUDIES – THE PROOF

Air bags are meant to be used in conjunction *with* seatbelts. If seatbelts are not used, air bags can cause severe injury or death. We need seatbelts to keep us from slamming into the air bags with unrestrained force (https://www.nhtsa.gov/vehicle-safety/seat-belts).

Dogs who ride on the driver's lap add an additional safety issue - **distraction**. They also block the driver's view of the speedometer, and physically prevent the driver from having unobstructed use of the steering wheel, turn signals, lights, and windshield wiper controls. Drivers cannot see their blind spot and do not have a clear view of their side mirrors.

"Loose pets inside of vehicles can become a deadly distraction for drivers." (https://www.americanhumane.org/public-education/remember-safety-while-driving-with-pets/)

Here are some interesting study results to consider:

"Volvo and The Harris Poll followed 15 drivers and their dogs for more than 30 hours on the road, to examine how driving with an unrestrained pet affected driving behavior vs. when an owner used restraints (e.g. pet seat belts, harnesses, crates, carriers). With pets allowed to roam freely, we found:

- Unsafe driving behaviors more than doubled; 649 instances while unrestrained vs. 274 while restrained.

- Includes climbing on a driver's lap or hanging their head out the window.

- Time drivers were distracted more than doubled; 3 hr. 39

min. unrestrained vs. 1 hr. 39 min. restrained.

- Includes dogs jumping from seat to seat or taking drivers' eyes off the road.

- Stress on both drivers and pups increased.

- Heart rates were likely to increase for people and pets.

- Unrestrained dogs measured a heart rate 7 beats per minute faster.

- Drivers felt calmer when dogs were buckled in, with heart rates dropping as much as 28 and 34 beats per minute (https://www.media.volvocars.com/us/en-us/media/press releases/256405/study-unrestrained-pets-increase-stress -and-distraction-on-the-road).

- Volvo and the Harris Poll also discovered that "77% of Americans say "people don't take vehicular dog safety seriously   enough (https://www.media.volvocars.com/us/en-us/media/docu mentfile/256407/keeping-pets-safe-on-the-road)."

STATE LAWS

It has taken a long time, during which so many dogs have been injured or killed, but many states are finally recommending that pet guardians utilize safety restraints when transporting dogs, and other animals, in vehicles.

Kudos to states who recognize the importance of keeping our beloved companion animals safe. Fines for unrestrained pets range up to $1000.00. Other states who do not have specific laws, utilize their laws for distracted drivers.

Many states consider unrestrained pets in a vehicle to be a violation of their animal cruelty laws. If that is not yet the case in your state, consider advocating for this important cause.

It takes so little money and effort to keep our pets safer.

Our dogs give us **all** that they are. They love whole-heartedly and unabashedly. They deserve our best in return.

Dog Park Dos and Don'ts

It has been over a decade since I first wrote this piece. We used to have an awesome time going to the dog park and we made cherished friends that we are still close with all these years later.

However, I no longer advise taking dogs to dog parks. This is my personal opinion, based on experiences we've had with out-of-control owners, and their dogs.

The risk to my dogs became too great.

DOG PARK DANGERS

DANGER #1: IRRESPONSIBLE OWNERS

One couple brought their large dogs to the dog park daily. As soon as they began to turn onto the long downhill road leading to the parking lot below, their dogs would jump out of the moving car's windows, go over or under the fence as fast as they could, and immediately try to dominate my dog.

Their owners had not even reached the parking lot by that time. Other park goers reported that the owners allowed this dangerous behavior every time.

Once they were finally parked, they'd slowly wander to the gates of the dog park. While they dawdled, I was faced with keeping their powerful dogs off my dog. I was responsible to keep her safe, and myself safe too.

Those people did not care about their dogs, other dogs, or people. My girl was social and docile. Thank goodness. However, she did not deserve to be forced into that situation every time those people showed up.

DANGER #2: DISEASES AND ILLNESS

A popular dog park in the area was shut down for most of an entire season due to an outbreak of ringworm. Then it was shut down again the next summer, and the next. Ringworm is a fungus that can be spread with direct contact, on contaminated objects like toys and water bowls, from infected rodents, and it can even live in the soil.

In addition to ringworm, many pathogens, viruses and bacteria can be concentrated in the small area of a busy dog park, increasing the chances of your dog becoming ill.

DANGER #3: ENVIRONMENTAL CONTAMINANTS

Many years ago, the city relented to requests from its citizens to allow a dog park. They created it in a retention basin where spring snowmelt drains in the spring, and summer rainstorms run off the mountain, creating a pond. It is not a location meant for a park. The city wanted to use it to gauge interest, to see if a dog park was popular enough to create a better, permanent one.

The park has been plagued with seasons of an overrun of tiny burrs, nearly impossible to get out of a dog's coat. It gets muddy. Algae grows. Mosquitoes breed and bite. The hillsides that have to be navigated to get into the park are so steep that they are a liability risk. Many elderly and disabled folks cannot use the park at all. There is no shade. Neighbors have fiercely opposed having the park near them and somehow forced the city to create parking bans on all public streets adjacent to the park. There is no parking lot.

I have avoided the dog park since early on, when the neighbors made parking in available shade impossible. I get extremely sick in high temperatures. I cannot park my car in the sun. Their mean-spirited and stubborn insistence feels like discrimination to me.

I'm glad our dogs have never been there.

In October 2025, a number of dogs were seen by a veterinarian for coughing, sneezing and respiratory distress. The veterinarian put the puzzle pieces together and found the common denominator in the lives of the dogs: they had all been to that same dog park.

The veterinarian's assessment: the dogs had inhaled deadly black mold that had grown in the bottom of the retention basin.

DANGER #4: DISTRACTION = DOG FIGHTS

Distraction plays a role in the many dog fights that break out. People are so attached to their screens that many are not aware of the energy and body language dynamics that are constantly changing in a dog park. It only takes one turn of a dog's head, or a lip lick, for a fight to break out.

The lag time between people hearing a fight, looking up from their screens to see what is going on, realizing that *their* dog is in the fight, standing up, running to their dog, and gaining control of their dog, takes far longer than it takes for serious injuries to occur, both to dogs and people.

DANGER #5: INJURIES AND VETERINARIAN BILLS

Many people take their dogs to the dog park for exercise. Of course the dogs run, play, and expend energy, but they are also at risk of accidental injury to bones, teeth, and soft tissue. The most innocent maneuver by overly excited dogs can create pain and big veterinarian bills. People can be easily bowled over and injured by running dogs too.

BETTER CHOICES

Auggie at the Silly Sunday Market in Park City, Utah©

BETTER CHOICE #1: WALKING SNIFFARIS

A better choice for exercise is structured adventure walks, including intermittent Sniffaris. I recommend walking at a brisk pace without stopping for 5-10 minutes at first, then allow them to stop and sniff for a minute or two, then pick up the pace for another round.

Brisk walking with you shifts their minds into working gear. You'll recognize it by the way they hold their ears; alert, and slightly back, bouncing along with their gait. If you are walking multiple dogs at once, with practice, they'll slip into working mode together. My soul *loves* to walk a pack of dogs in this mode. It is pure enjoyment for all of us.

Sniffing nurtures dogs in many ways. Humans interpret the world mainly by sight. Dogs interpret their world mainly by scent.

"Dogs devote lots of brain power to interpreting smells. They have more than 100 million sensory receptor sites in the nasal cavity compared to 6 million in people, and the area of the canine brain devoted to analyzing odors is about 40 times larger than the comparable part of the human brain." (Hunter, Llera, Buzhardt, 2024)   (https://vcahospitals.com/know-your-pet/how-dogs-use-smell-to-perceive-the-world#)

Sniffing provides mental stimulation as they read and interpret the world through scent. It also calms their minds and emotions by activating the parasympathetic nervous system, providing relaxation and stress reduction.

Walking together, working together, and allowing dogs to sniff make for a wonderful bonding activity with exercise as an added benefit. Dog parks allow dogs to get excited and run together, but they do not provide meaningful interaction, relaxation, stress reduction and bonding like walks do.

BETTER CHOICE #2: CURATED PLAY DATES

Play time with other reliable dogs (monitored by reliable owners) can be great fun. A carefully curated play date can be an awesome experience for all. These usually take place in private yards where dogs and owners know each other and know that the dogs are compatible, healthy and vaccinated.

DOG PARK DOS

If you choose to take your dogs to the dog park, here are some basic guidelines to follow, all intended to keep you and your dogs safe. Be *sure* to read the rules posted at each park.

TIP #1: CRITICAL SKILL-MAKE *SURE* YOUR DOG HAS A SOLID, RELIABLE RECALL

Your dog needs to have a bomb-proof recall skill that they will respond to immediately, no matter what is going on around them, in all circumstances. When called, they need to be willing and able to stop whatever they are doing instantly, and come straight to you without hesitation, distraction or question.

Dogs do not learn recall at a dog park. It is a skill that must be mastered over time, through focused training and thorough proofing in variable situations.

A RELIABLE RECALL SAVES LIVES, not just at the park, but everywhere. If you and your dog have not yet mastered the recall, get to work on it, using *positive* training methods.

NEVER yell at your dog, especially when they are coming TOWARD you! That is the time to praise and encourage them to continue coming to your side, even if it took them a while to get started in your direction. Upbeat, happy praise will make them more likely to come to you sooner the next time you call.

TIP #2: PLEASE TEACH THE CHILDREN IN YOUR LIFE THESE RULES TO KEEP THEM, AND THE DOGS THEY ENCOUNTER, SAFE

This may be tough to hear, but do not take children to the dog park. It is for ***dogs***.

Dogs-at-play, running full-speed, get rowdy and exuberant. Children can become injured easily, and completely by accident. No one wants to see children get hurt, or see dogs end up in quarantine at the animal shelter, due to a bite incident that is 100% preventable.

TIP #3: VACCINATIONS

That's right, I said the "V" word. It is paramount that you do not take an unvaccinated dog to a dog park! As the human in this scenario, it is *your responsibility* to make sure your dog is current on all of their vaccinations, licensed in your city (if required), and microchipped. Make sure that you *register* that microchip and include all of your contact information. A microchip only matters if your contact information will pop up if your pet is scanned for one. Make sure your dog is healthy before going to the park.

TIP #4: DO NOT APPROACH DOGS WHO DON'T YET KNOW YOU

Dogs will come to you when they feel safe. Keep your hands, your body and your mind relaxed and neutral. Dogs are *experts* at reading body language and energy. ***Ignore*** them. Allow them to come to you if they want to. Don't stick your hand out for them to sniff. That is *asking* for a dog bite. We wouldn't like someone to rudely stick their hand in our face; dogs don't like it either.

TIP #5: NEVER ALLOW YOUR DOGS, OR YOUR CHILDREN, TO RUN UP TO A STRANGE DOG!

Yelling, "Don't worry, he's friendly!" will not stop a dog fight from kicking off, or from over-excited dogs tangling up humans in leashes, jumping, nipping, or knocking you down.

Ignore dogs until they approach you.

Follow the safety rules of **No Touch, No Talk, No Eye-contact**.

TIP #6: NO TOUCH, NO TALK, NO EYE-CONTACT

Why no eye-contact? Because that is the most aggressive, dominant, action you can take and many dogs feel intimidated or threatened by direct extended eye-contact. They do not enjoy being stared down any more than you do.

Why no touch, including sticking your hand out for a dog to sniff it? Because reaching for them before they are ready feels intrusive to them, perhaps even frightening. They may feel their only option is to bite, to get you to back up out of their personal space. It is up to humans to prevent these situations.

Why no talk? Because it is added noise, which can increase excitement, which can lead to unwanted, even dangerous, outcomes.

Often, when people approach a strange dog, they make eye-contact, stick their fingers in the dog's face to sniff, and talk in a high-pitched, excited, voice that only accomplishes amping up the energy, and perhaps anxiety, in the dog.

Just imagine if we ran up to human strangers, stared them down, stuck our hands in their faces, and tittered away in a high-pitched nonsensical language! We can imagine the reaction we'd receive. It would certainly be negative.

Yet, people expect dogs to like these intrusive behaviors that we would not allow to be done to us.

Empathy is a factor here. Consider it *all* from the dog's point of view. The result would be fewer nervous dogs, and fewer bites.

Pearlie: My Service Dog©

My service dog, Pearlie, did not like strangers staring into her eyes. I understood their fascination - she had absolutely gorgeous eyes. She never broke eye-contact with the rude starers, even though they made her uncomfortable.

Strangers would walk up to us, interrupt us as we tried to complete an errand on what meager amount of energy I may have had that day. Many would try to make intense, prolonged eye-contact with her, then say to me, "Wow. She looks uncomfortable."

No kidding! Of course she looked uncomfortable!

It was always said to me in a shaming sort of way, as though Pearlie and I were the interrupting offenders. I would place my body between them and her, to block their stares and protect my girl, who was working hard to protect my health. There were many rude people who I had to instruct to back up and leave us alone.

TIP #7: KNOW DOG BODY LANGUAGE

Never reach over the top of a strange dog's head or neck. And watch for signs of discomfort in your own dogs. They may duck a little, tighten up their facial muscles, pin their ears back, or lick their lips. These are all signs that a dog does not like it, and if pushed, could lead to a bite.

Those warning signs are all direct communication from dog to human, telling us that they feel uncomfortable or even threatened. They are telling us to give them space.

Dogs don't have thumbs, they can't spell it out in a note or a text, they use every signal they have available to warn before they feel forced to use the only defense they have - their teeth.

It is *our responsibility* to pay attention to what they are telling us.

TIP #8: PROPER LEASH USE

Always have your dog on a leash (never a flexi-leash, they are dangerous) when out in public, including your approach to the dog park. Loose dogs in the parking lot are in danger of being injured or killed. Use common sense.

The time to remove the leash is once you and your dog are safely inside the second gate.

Close the first gate behind you, before opening the second one.

TIP #9: PROPER ENTRY PROCEDURE

ALWAYS enter each gate to the park, and the park itself, BEFORE your dog does. This sets the tone, and is good practice when allowing your dog through any door, any gate, any threshold. Even at home. It is important for them to follow you, rather than lead.

This practice lets your dog know that you have the situation under control, and that they can feel calm, rather than worry about being in charge of a place or situation. It is better for them, not just us.

TIP #10: ONCE INSIDE THE DOG PARK

Take your dog's leash off immediately after entering the dog park. Leashes can create tension and overexcitement. Your dog will be excited to go to the other dogs at play, and those dogs will also come up to your dog for greetings.

Leash tension can negatively affect the energy of the entire park pack, which can result in fights & injuries.

If your dog does not have perfect, proofed, recall, do not take them to the dog park.

If your dog is not reliable off-leash, do not take them to the dog park.

If your dog is not well-socialized with dogs, and humans, do not take them to the dog park.

If your dog is not healthy, or is not vaccinated, do not take them to the dog park.

TIP #11: NO SCREENS

Leave your screens out of the park. Turn off your phone and the outside world. Be present! Take every opportunity you can to connect, *really connect*, with your dog.

Keep your energy calm, positive, upbeat and engaged. The dogs will *all* love you for it!

TIP #12: DOG PARK DOO-DOO

Always pick up your dog's waste. ALWAYS. A kind courtesy is to pick up after your own dog, and two others. That helps keep the dog park as clean as possible. Everyone benefits.

Dog parks aren't for *every* dog.

But carefully curated puppy parties, combined with excellent nutrition, fresh water, daily adventure walks, sniffaris, plenty of exercise, and fun training activities add up to a balanced, content, and well-socialized pup.

My Seizure Alert Princesses

Pearlie: Out to Lunch with Us © Mariesa Galloway

When people met Pearlie, my red-nosed brindle American Pit Bull Terrier (APBT), and learned that she alerted me prior to the beginning of a seizure, their first question was, "How does she know that you're going to have a seizure?"

I didn't know the answer at the time. I only knew how grateful I was for her reliability to alert me. I am forever thankful for her willingness to be by my side, keeping continual watch, as my faithful service dog.

Next, people asked how I got her and where she was trained. Many inquired about the cost also, especially if they knew someone who might benefit from the assistance of a service dog.

That is where the miraculous story of my seizure alert princesses, Pearlie (named Princess prior to adoption), and our Rottweiler, Prinzessin Sadie, began.

Neither of them were service dogs at the start, they each began as pets. But they soon revealed their true skills and purpose.

I always say that God sends the right dog at the right time. Sadie and Pearlie are proof.

One day, several years before Pearlie arrived, Sadie, our Rottweiler, began staring at me intensely. Her expressive face, and tilted head, told me she was concerned and she was trying to help me understand what was wrong.

Sadie was intelligent, and loyal. She knew the names of all of her toys. Guests were amazed that I could ask her to get a specific toy out of dozens and she would bring the right one every time. She had a repertoire of tricks.

Sadie and I had "conversations" throughout each day. When I spoke, she would make eye contact and tilt her beautiful head back and forth like she understood every word. Our communication was not simply my giving a command and Sadie obeying it. It was more like talking with a friend and feeling understood. I tried to make her feel understood too by asking questions until she showed me what she wanted. She was incredible.

She also had an exceptional sense of humor. When my husband and I would leave the house, I would tell her, "Be a good girl and take good care of things. We will be back soon."

Most of the time she would do exactly that. Other times, we would return to a little surprise left for us in a doorway in the house. Sadie would steal one item from one of us, and carefully leave it in a doorway.

We kept the house clean and always wondered how she managed to find and steal the things she did. The items were never destroyed, or even wet from slobber. Sadie was delicate in her silent protests. We might come home to a pen, or a golf score card, or a paper on the floor. She would greet us with an innocent face and a whole-body wiggle, from snout to stubby tail.

One day, we returned to find nothing on the floor, but to Sadie asking for help. She was holding her mouth kind of oddly so I checked to see what she might be hiding.

To our surprise, she had Fixodent stuck throughout her teeth like she was planning to put in a set of doggie dentures! She patiently let me remove it all then thanked me with a big grin and a kiss. Thankfully, Fixodent did not have any toxic sweeteners in it like most toothpastes have. She wasn't injured. And she never did that again, a credit to her intelligence.

Sadie was a quick learner. We hung a jingle bell on the door and she would ring it each time she wanted to go outside. When we gave her a new toy, we would give it a name. She usually remembered it after the first introduction, and definitely after the second.

As a puppy, I once asked her if she was thirsty. From that day forward, to her, the word "thirsty" meant a drink of water. To humans, it may have sounded ridiculous for me to ask, "Sadie, do you want a thirsty?" But that was her language for it.

We could spell ride or walk, but it didn't help. She figured that out right away.

She was good at understanding us, and we *thought* we were good at understanding her.

One afternoon, Sadie sat down, facing me as I sat on the couch. She was making intense eye-contact, never looking away.

I started going through the list of questions to see what she might need or want: "Do you want a thirsty? A puzzle? Blue, red, orange (names of toys)? Do you want to go outside? Do you want to go for a walk?"

She did not get excited about any of the options. She just looked at me and sighed.

I did not understand what she was trying to tell me.

Sadie settled on the floor by my feet for a few minutes.

I returned to reading. But then I felt the couch shake.

I'd never taught her to "beg" by sitting on her hind end and raising her upper body into the typical beg position. Yet, that day she suddenly sat upright on the floor facing me, and began to pound the frame at the end of the love seat. She rocked back and forth, hitting it with her front paws. She was relentless; not destructive, but determined to get me to understand that there was something urgent going on.

She must have thought I was the least intelligent being alive. I had no clue what she meant, or what I needed to do.

Sadie was an obedient girl who would usually settle down when I asked. But that day, she let me know that *she knew best*. She didn't stop until I made eye-contact with her, to *connect* with her, and told her that I understood she was trying to tell me something important. "What is it sweet girl? What's wrong?"

After she felt she had truly been seen and heard, she would settle down, then repeat the behavior a few moments later.

We repeated the same type of communication many times. I wanted to understand, but didn't. I don't remember how many months, or longer, it took me to figure out what she was trying so diligently to tell me.

During that time, I became ill. The energy I normally had in the mornings disappeared. I had been working more than full-time selling real estate and helping to recruit and train new agents. I commuted an hour to work and back. I started each day by leaving home at 4:00 a.m. to get to the gym at 5:00 a.m., worked out for an hour, got cleaned up and dressed up and to the office for our 7:30 a.m. mindset meeting. I worked a full day and commuted home with enough energy left to make dinner, play with the dogs, visit my grandma, tidy the house, spend time with my husband and get ready to repeat it all the next day.

Suddenly, I was mired in an exhaustion that was debilitating. I now know that it was neurological fatigue which is not like normal tiredness. It doesn't go away or get better with a good night's sleep. It can be cumulative, as it was in my case. There was no relief from it.

I had to drop the workouts because I couldn't wake up and get out of the house in time. I was too exhausted for any physical exertion. Then I started missing our 7:30 meeting. I would drag into the office at whatever time I could finally make it there. I started rearranging appointments with clients, which was troubling to me. I had always been reliable.

My new normal was that I was becoming "reliably unreliable." Once in the office, I would shut my door, close the blinds, lay down on the floor and sleep however many hours it took until I could wake up and commute home. I get emotional thinking back because it was such a helpless, hopeless feeling, not knowing what was wrong, not knowing what to do about it, and wondering if that was all my life was going to be. I was only 35 years old.

I started having odd, intermittent symptoms. My speech would get jumbled, I blurted sounds and words because my mouth and throat would spasm. My thinking became foggy. I couldn't look at certain textures or the episodes would begin. I started to have an electrical, tingling, sensation in the top of my head that felt like it came from my brain. That feeling would be accompanied by snippets of images that played in my mind like a movie.

The physical sensation and the images that felt like memories, but were déjà vu. They would start out fairly weak, then grow in intensity with each round until a crescendo was reached at their strongest point. Then they would begin to diminish in strength until, after several more rounds, they would stop. All of it was worse, and more intense, during times of higher stress. I wondered if I was having migraines.

For the first time in my life, I was having seizures. I never lost consciousness, but my mind was fuzzy. I didn't have the kind of seizures that include big physical movements. The episodes left me exhausted.

Looking back, it all makes sense. Sadie was incredibly sensitive, and that must have included the changes that occurred in my body prior to a round of seizures. I didn't connect her alerts to my seizures, because she notified me well in advance, sometimes 24-48 hours in advance. And once the seizures began, my mind became hazy and foggy, so I didn't link up the connection after the seizures left me either.

It was a couple of years after she began alerting me that my neurologist diagnosed and treated them.

The day it clicked and I realized the connection, I was in absolute awe of how precious and powerful our Creator made the bond between human and canine.

I didn't teach Sadie how to recognize the changes in my body that meant a seizure was looming. I did not know what they were. She was a natural alerter. She knew long before I did that something was wrong.

Sadie taught me. She was 100% reliable with her alerts.

Many years after Sadie's first alert, Pearlie (then named Princess) came to visit for a weekend. She was only a year old. She'd had little socialization, spending most of her days locked in a bathroom. She was surprisingly well-behaved in our home, however. She and

Sadie got along well. I expected them to play together and enjoy walks. I did not expect Sadie to begin to mentor and train her intensely.

At times, Pearlie would initiate play and Sadie would respond joyfully. Other times, Sadie would rebuke the invitation. She would draw Pearlie's focus to me by making huffing noises, acting extra excited, and performing her alerting behavior of pounding the end of the couch with her front paws. That made Pearlie curious. I can only imagine her thinking Sadie had lost her marbles, that they'd never played that weird game before. Pearlie loved excitement, however, and her energy would amp up in its presence.

Sadie's urgency and antics kept and held Pearlie's attention. Pearlie wanted to understand the rules of the new game.

I don't know how to speak the language of dogs. Thankfully Pearlie did. She quickly caught on to what Sadie was doing and why.

I kept telling Sadie to relax, that Pearlie was just a guest for the weekend.

Once again, I didn't understand what our brilliant Sadie was up to.

A few months later, Princess's family called. They were moving and said they could not take her with them. They asked if we would take her and find her a good home. They were on their way to surrender her to the animal shelter as we spoke on the phone.

We agreed to help. She was very fearful and shy around strangers. I knew she would never get adopted out of the shelter. She would be traumatized and euthanized.

I had three great families in mind for her. But as soon as she arrived, Sadie began showing her the ropes with focused intensity. It was strange and beautiful and out of my hands.

None of the families were interested in Princess. Unexpectedly, to us, Pearlie became a member of our family.

It was *right* for her to be with us. Sadie made that evident.

Only eight months after Pearlie's arrival, our sweet Sadie passed away. Her work was through. She made sure Pearlie understood that she was supposed to keep a close watch on me, detect the warning signs of a pending seizure, and alert me before they hit.

Pearlie had her own way of alerting me, different from Sadie's method. She put her front paws up on my legs, or chair, so she could reach my head to nuzzle my left temple. She only did that pre-seizure and never at any other time.

The first MRI of my brain showed a large lesion in the area she always pointed to. It was divine affirmation that Pearlie was meant to be with me.

Though their alerting methods were different , their purpose was the same. Pearlie, like her mentor, Sadie, was 100% reliable.

Multiple Sclerosis has changed many things in my life. It made me hesitant and untrusting of my body. Twenty-years post-diagnosis, it still does. But the blessings of Sadie and Pearlie gave me back a great deal of independence, of feeling safe when venturing out in the world. I gained confidence and became less fearful.

It's true there can be beauty for ashes. Sadie's urn, and Pearlie's too, both quote God's promise given in Revelation 21: 5. "Behold! I make **all** things new!"

This promise gives me so much hope because it is a declaration that God will fulfill a complete renewal of **all** creation. I believe this includes not just humans, but the companion animals we love so dearly, and who love us in return.

I rely on God's promises. He is faithful. He keeps His word. I look forward in faith to the day I will once again snuggle and play with the many beloved dogs I've lost during my lifetime.

I can't wait to pet Pearlie's velvety ears, watch her spin and run zoomies in glee, and see Sadie tilt her head at the sound of my voice again. I can't wait to hear her Rotti "grumbles" and see her do her little dance, tapping her hind feet, one at a time, and swaying from side to side as I scratch her back above her hips; her favorite spot.

I'm thankful for the little bit of heaven on earth I enjoyed because of Sadie's and Pearlie's loyal, generous, and trustworthy work. They were heaven-sent.

I don't fully understand the science of how dogs detect seizure activity, but I'm thankful I invested the effort to understand their behavior, their ways of communicating, and learned to trust their instincts. Thankfully, I no longer have seizures, another inexplicable turn of events on my MS journey.

My heart is filled with gratitude for my Seizure Alert Princesses.

Pearlie and Sadie ©

The Gift of Now

Ace: Our Fluffy Friend©

Imagine the tremendous amount of time we humans spend worrying about a past that we cannot change and future concerns that may or may not happen. When added up, that time consumes a major portion of our lives - time that cannot be regained, and time that could have been spent in immensely more enjoyable ways.

It's concerning to consider in its entirety - in days, months, and years - gone from the limited time we've been given.

Our companion animals give us their unfailing, unconditional love. They also give us a priceless gift that we cannot always manufacture for ourselves. They give us the gift of living in the *now*.

Dogs focus on the present moment and situation. They function in accordance with our current energy and actions. They respond as needed - when needed.

When we head out for a walk, I am confident that I am the only one ruminating over something in the past, or worrying over, or planning, something for the future.

My pups are simply enjoying the walk! They sniff the breeze, and the grass. They notice ducks, and squirrels with delight, and let their tongues flop out of their happy faces at random. What a joyous, low-stress, way to live!

I want to learn from them. I want to simply accept and enjoy the daily gifts they give me from their end of the leash; the lesson of living exuberantly in the *now*.

Instead of worrying about chores, phone calls, tasks and meetings, I want to notice what the mountains that surround us look like right at that very second. I want to truly see the sunset, with all its breathtaking hues and the depths and dimensions of the clouds. I want to hear our combined footfalls on the path of our journey, our time together on Earth.

I want to notice everything that I have been pushing into the background, instead of giving time and energy to worry, stress and anxiety.

I want to create space to breathe, to feel my heart beat. I want to feel connected, instead of distracted. I want to experience every precious moment fully and vibrantly. I want to live in the now, and let the rest go.

It is my hope that you will also accept the gift your companion animals desperately want you to receive.

Let's join them in the *now*, walking in step *with* them, *fully present.*

A Tribute to Horses as Companions

Baby Lawrence (8 months old): Our Friend,
Ann's, Equine Companion of a Lifetime.
(Photographer Unknown)

Each July in Utah, residents celebrate the arrival of the Mormon pioneers. Our attention turns to parades, rodeos and fairs. Horses abound as we are reminded of our roots in the wild west frontier, and of the crucial roles horses played, not only in settling the west, but as early companion animals also.

Before western Native Americans began to acquire the "Big Dog" or "Sacred Dog" in the late 1500s, nomadic tribes carried their belongings on foot or with the help of dogs who were equipped with packs and travois.

To Indigenous Peoples, the arrival of the Spanish horse gave them mobility and a drastic improvement to their way of life. Simply put, the tribes with horses dominated those tribes without. The horse made it possible to hunt more easily, and to trade excess buffalo meat and hides for guns, cloth, glass beads and metal tools.

The horse as a companion animal transformed the rider into a creature with the thought process and imagination of a human, combined with the grass-fueled power, speed, and agility of a horse.

"Such a person had become one of those mythical creatures, a centaur, half-man and half-stallion," wrote N. Scott Momaday in The Names, a memoir, and in reference to the Kiowas, his people. "They became centaurs of the spirit."

Horses have always tended to the spirit of humankind. The horse symbol, often featured in ancient pictograms, signified not just the physical attributes of mobility, stamina, strength and power, but also certain matters of the heart, including loyalty, devotion, love and mutual respect.

The Creator gave us a magnificent teacher, and ally of the spirit, when He gave us the horse.

Lawrence (34 years old) with Ann: Best Friends for Life ©Shelly Shipley

Hope's Rescue

Hope was a tiny Chihuahua who was gravely injured after being thrown into a fire pit. Her rescuers fought for her life. Tragically, she succumbed to those injuries.

Little Hope inspired a group of people with huge hearts to form a rescue organization named in her honor. In January 2013, Hope's last breath breathed life into Hope's Rescue. Hope's legacy lives on.

Based in Ogden, UT, this group of dedicated volunteers has one goal: to save as many lives as possible. Homeless animals are pulled from local shelters and placed in loving foster homes.

Each animal receives appropriate medical care including vaccinations, spay or neuter, and a microchip. The ultimate goal is to adopt each precious companion animal into their forever home.

Hope's Rescue makes a lifelong commitment to each of their precious dogs and cats. Even terminally ill animals are provided loving and dignified care through Hope's Rescue Hospice Program.

***

2025 Update: I first met some of the wonderful volunteers from Hope's Rescue, and wrote about the organization eleven years ago, in 2014. I'm happy to report that they are still going strong, saving animals who are in deep need of loving, forever homes.

They also operate their hospice program, helping animals receive care and compassion in the last season of life in a home, rather than at a shelter. Hope's Rescue pays for all of the medical care and supplies needed for the rest of their lives.

They make such a tremendous difference for companion animals.

Many of the caring volunteers that I met in 2014 are still saving the lives of companion animals. They have my deep respect and gratitude. They all work to ensure that these dear animals never see the inside of a shelter again.

To learn more about adopting, fostering, or donating, and to see animals currently available through Hope's Rescue, please visit https://www.facebook.com/HopesRescue.Utah

Hope's Hospice

Every day, once-beloved pets are surrendered to shelters because their owners will no longer care for them when they become aged or ill.

Imagine the pain, emotionally and physically, that these dear companion animals experience at an extremely vulnerable time in their lives, discarded by their family at their greatest time of need.

Hope's Rescue (https://www.facebook.com/HopesRescue.Utah) has a special heart, and hospice program, to help these dear animals.

Hope's Rescue has amazing foster families, true angels, who volunteer to foster pets who, without them, would have no chance of being adopted from a shelter. These wonderful fosters take in sweet souls who desperately need to be in a home.

Hope's Rescue provides the funding for their care, including all veterinary expenses. Rather than sitting alone and bewildered in a noisy shelter, these pets become beloved companions once again, living out the remainder of their lives in dignity and love.

It is always difficult to say goodbye to someone we treasure. There is also no feeling more satisfying than knowing you have saved an adoring heart who someone else just threw away.

When it comes time to say goodbye, these rescued companions do not have to go through it alone; a volunteer from Hope's Rescue is there to hold and comfort them.

Hospice fostering is important and deeply rewarding work. It means a sweet pet does not have to die alone and confused. They are held in the arms of love and compassion.

They are deeply grateful for everything that is done for them, from the first day they enter your home, until they breathe their last breath.

Foster homes are needed today! Will you open your heart and home to one of these special angels? They have so much unconditional love, gratitude and joy to give in return.

Search for rescue organizations in your area for more information about their individual programs. Or contact Hope's Hospice at the link above.

"You're never too old to love, and to be loved." ~ Anonymous

Purrfect Pawprints

Three words describe the wonderful volunteers at Purrfect Paw-prints: laser-focused, and busy.

They are laser-focused on helping to create a world where animals don't die anymore just because they are frivolously tossed aside. They volunteer countless hours to rescue, spay, neuter, foster, love and find forever homes for precious companion animals.

When I first wrote about Purrfect Pawprints in 2014, they had been helping animals since 2008. They had already spayed or neutered nearly 5,000 animals in that brief period of time.

The veterinarian who helps them is over 70-miles, one-way, from their location. That adds up to a 12-hour day for the volunteers by the time they pick up the fur babies, transport them to the veterinarian for surgery, then transport them home again.

In 2008 they were looking to procure a reliable vehicle for the organization for transport trips. Dedicated volunteers do all of this compassionate work on their own time and on their own dime.

Their main message is PLEASE SPAY AND NEUTER YOUR PETS.

So much suffering and death could be avoided if humans would prevent litters from occurring.

Cats and dogs don't become better behaved because they have one litter before being spayed. That is a complete myth.

There are resources available for low-cost altering options, like vouchers from Best Friends, the Humane Society, local rescue organizations and animal shelters.

What are some other ways you can help? Open your heart and home. Foster, foster, foster! Why is fostering so critical? The equation is literally one-for-one.

For every companion animal that is lovingly taken into a foster home, room is made in the shelter for another animal.

Fostering saves lives in a very direct way.

When shelters are full, innocent animals are euthanized. That is the sad reality that Jamie Carter Park witnessed day in and day out as a former animal control officer in northern Utah.

"I rescue because I've seen the shelter situation first hand...animals [euthanized] who could have potentially been saved in a world with less unwanted animals and more resources. I want to create that world," she said.

Foster and rescue work takes a lot of heart. Love abounds with Purrfect Pawprints.

"You can't always cope with the heartache. Sometimes you go through an intense mourning process that lasts for months. But you can use that to drive you as you work to help others," said Jamie Carter Park.

"It always helps to know that the furbaby passed in a home and got to experience love. They didn't die alone in a cage," said Ann Marie Fuller.

For more info on fostering, adopting, helping, or donating, please visit purrfectpawprints.org

Maddie's Makeover

Maddie©

Maddie weighs barely ten pounds and is full of attitude and joy. Betty had been searching for a nice little dog. At the right time and circumstance, Maddie came into Betty's life.

While caring for her husband who suffered with Alzheimer's disease, Betty hoped to find just the right little dog, one who would brighten her husband's declining days at the Veteran's nursing home. And she knew her own loneliness and sorrow would be eased with some canine company.

Tommy and Betty had been caring guardians of several dogs over the years, Betty said it felt odd for them to be without. She asked if we would help her in her search.

After an almost year-long search,and considering the many wonderful homeless dogs available, we wondered why hadn't we found that special One?

Then an email arrived. As with others, it simply read that there may be a match to our inquiries. A photo appeared. A small black and white Shih-tzu blend with black, sparkling eyes.

Betty took one look at the picture and wanted to meet Maddie right away. Would we be able to see her? Would she still be available?

We rushed to the shelter, hoping we were not too late. The staff sent me into the back, into the kennels. I dreaded going back there. I knew it would hurt my heart to see all of those hopeful faces, knowing I could not take them all home.

I steeled my resolve. I was doing this to help a friend. I looked very carefully through the kennels, one by one, and was disheartened when I reached the last kennel and there was no sight of her. The dog we had hoped for was missing.

Had someone adopted her? The shelter staff was sure she was back there. I double-checked the last kennel. It looked empty. But there she was! She was far smaller than she'd appeared in her photo and she had been curled up, hiding in the shadows.

I sat on the floor, trying to make myself look as small as possible, so that this tiny dog would not feel intimidated, then opened the door. She made eye-contact with me and began rubbing her body back and forth, crawling submissively, along the kennel wall.

After four or five roundtrips of that, she inched forward toward me and flopped over onto her back. She showed me her belly and accepted a gentle belly rub.

I took her into the lobby to meet Betty. It was love at first sight.

Some believe that when a person and a dog need each other, our Creator makes the match at the right time. I'm a believer, having witnessed that many times in my own life, and in others'.

There were concerns and questions, of course. What was Maddie's story? How did this tiny girl find herself at an animal shelter?

We were told she was rescued while wandering alone during a snowstorm. Her long hair was matted to the skin and pressed painful puncture weeds into her tender flesh.

A before photo showed her *terrible* condition upon rescue. But she had tolerated a full grooming and nail trim.

I drove Betty and Maddie home, praying for the best. Maddie had, in a matter of days, moved from suffering alone in the streets, to the shelter, to Betty's arms. That first night, Maddie snuggled on a pillow after fluffing it up to her satisfaction. She slept soundly through the night.

Could life get any better?

Within days, the two were a bonded pair. Maddie took her care-giving very seriously, keeping a watchful eye on Betty and their home. Maddie helped to fill it with love and laughter.

***

Those of us who rescue know we saved our animal companions from a terrible fate. These amazing rescued companions truly rescue us as well.

Lexi

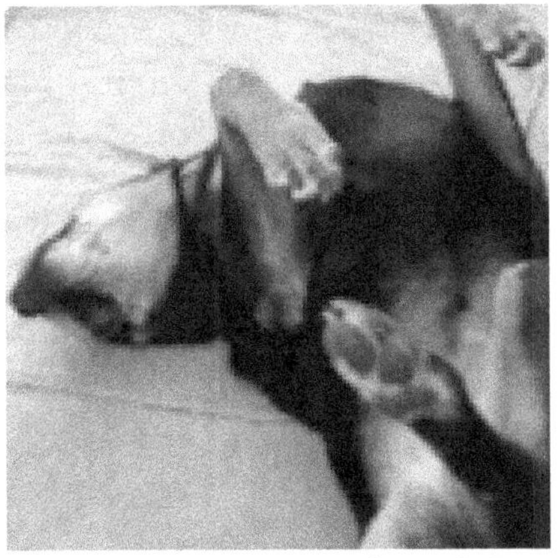

Lexi: Sweet Tri-Pawed Rotti, En-joying Life!©

Lexi arrived like a supercell summer thunderstorm; a Rottweiler who became an instant family member.

And family project.

Raised in a drug house filled with violence and volatility, Lexi had a low self-esteem that she tried to hide by acting overly boisterous and tough.

But when she was approached to be petted and loved on, she was too shy, too tenderhearted, too uncertain, to lift her giant head off the carpet to be petted. Our goal was to help her grow in confidence and self-esteem.

We approached her with assurance, telling her what a good girl she was. We gently lifted her chin off the floor to stroke her velvety ears, soothing her, and hoping to give her a semblance of security and peace.

Lexi allowed us to do this. She *wanted* to be loved like that.

As the weeks passed, a new Lexi evolved. Her confidence grew. We learned that she adored children, and was a comedian with a great sense of humor.

It was such a joy to watch her true personality emerge. It took her several days to decompress, many weeks to feel safe enough to let her guard down, and many months for her to come out of her protective shell.

Lexi's bark was loud, *epically* loud. Her voice turned heads, rattled windows, reverberated up and down the block, and rocked the car during rides.

Her bite, however, was reserved only for kibble and toys.

Inside her deep chest beat a gentle, courageous heart.

Lexi's health issues first manifested in the form of a bump on her hind leg, below the hock joint.

The first veterinarian we consulted thought that it was likely some synovial fluid, a viscous fluid that lubricates and cushions joints.

I desperately hoped he was right.

My intuition was screaming that wasn't the answer.

The second veterinarian we consulted felt it was more than synovial fluid. He aspirated it, and checked the sample under the microscope at the clinic. He looked concerned when he told me he didn't recognize the cells he was seeing.

Next, he did a biopsy and sent it to the laboratory at the College of Veterinary Medicine & Biomedical Sciences at Colorado State University in Fort Collins, CO. The results were *devastating.*

It was the rarest, fastest spreading, and deadliest form of cancer they'd seen. They felt it was due to the drugs that she had been exposed to in her prior house.

I can't call that a *home.*

Amputation was the only way to save her life. It was a difficult but necessary decision. She was in good health otherwise, and she was just coming out of her shell, out of her trauma, and gaining momentum on living her *best* bold life.

She was a young dog with a bright future. And we were head over heels in love with her.

We prayed for the best outcome. God delivered.

Between the few days that the veterinarian sent in the biopsy and the near-emergency amputation procedure, the tumor had grown from below her hock to nearly the top of her hip!

A few more days would have meant no treatment, no cure. It would have been too late.

The veterinarian came in on his day off to successfully remove her 18-pound, cancer-riddled leg. We prayed that he was able to remove all of the cancer from her body.

When Lexi first came home from the veterinarian, it looked as though she thought she had no back legs at all. She didn't realize that she still had her other powerful leg.

We were heartbroken for her. We berated ourselves for putting her through the surgery.

We had to come up with some solutions quickly to help her move, to go outside to potty, to learn that she still had three legs and that she could walk.

We devised slings out of bath towels to help hold her up. Moving her was a two-person job. Before the surgery, she weighed in at 118 pounds.

Lexi was extremely independent. She fought to live, and to regain her mobility. She wanted it as much as we did.

A few days after surgery, she discovered that her healthy hind leg still worked! The discovery was evident in her expression. She was so excited! She stabilized her back end, and we cautiously dropped the sling. She stood in her own strength!

It was miraculous to watch her grow stronger, to gain better balance, to walk on the front end and hop on the back. A little 4-year old friend watched her one day and exclaimed with delight, "Her's *skipping*!!"

Her words were perfect. Lexi did indeed look like she was skipping! Perhaps like a freight train engine barreling down a track, but skipping, nonetheless.

With every step she became stronger, better balanced, and faster. She developed confidence and better self-esteem.

Lexi's heart beat to a new cadence. She enjoyed life with every ounce of her. Every day. She took *great* pleasure in even the little things.

In retrospect, would our family adopt another dog with special needs? Absolutely!

Lexi was a special spirit who taught us to accept life as it occurs, and to live every moment of our lives with joy and gratitude.

"But You, O Lord, are a shield for me, my glory and

the One who *lifts up my head*.~ Psalm 3:3

Lexi Wading in the River, Sniffing the Breeze & the Trees. ©

Canine Companions Elevate Park City

Park City went to the dogs long ago, in a great way. They add to "Bark City's" charm, as only their furry, friendly faces can. Through its boom or bust history, the dogs of Park City have grown in popularity and expanded their roles.

There are business-minded pups, like the giant Newfoundland Retrievers, "The Boys," that run the Love Your Pet Bakery. And mascot rescue dog, Fletcher, of Fletcher's restaurant. Park City Avalanche Dogs work hard to rescue or recover avalanche victims. These expert life savers train vigorously and continually, on and off the ski slopes, to be ready when duty calls.

Monty, the Bernese Mountain dog, is the official ambassador at Montage, a luxury resort; an excellent four-star, four-pawed perk. Each Labor Day weekend, the best sheepdogs in the world come to show their top-notch work at the Soldier Hollow Sheepdog Classic. Your circle of canine friends may expand on any stroll up Main Street.

Dogs are inspiration and icon. This town caters to its hounds. Dog parks offer dog-party fun. Pet boutiques offer necessities and accessories.

Every dog has her day in October. The Howl-o-ween activities include a parade where the town's dogs strut their stuff in costumes.

The Silly Sunday Market is a weekly dog-friendly celebration and farmer's market throughout the summer.

The town abounds with restaurants that provide patio seating and bowls of water for canine companions. There are walking and hiking services, even a masseuse.

One doggie day care offers pick-up service in its canine-customized school bus. What more can a pup ask for?

Dogs are art, displayed on the moose sculpture in front of the bike shop. And celebrated, as part of the past exhibit Park City Pets: Our Lives with Animals, at the Park City Museum. They are cherished, rescued, and adopted.

A local rescue organization, Nuzzles & Co, has saved thousands of lives over the past 25 years.

Dogs have it made in "Bark City." Its hounds elevate the town.

Hugo©

One of the first Park City pups that visitors will encounter is Hugo. His happy face is the logo for his namesake, Hugo Coffee. The canine vibe is present from the parking lot to the patio. Since Hugo's shop shares space with the Park City Kimball Junction & Visitor Information Center, dogs are allowed to come inside and hang out with their humans in one of several cozy seating areas.

First time visitors smile when they spot Hugo's mug on bags of coffee, artwork and merchandise. They know they have arrived in an amazing place.

And if his Pibble pals Ari and Monkey happen to be there, guests get an extra-exuberant greeting.

Hugo's mom, Claudia McMullin, was the former executive director of the Friends of Animals Utah rescue organization (now Nuzzles & Co.). That is where the pair met. Hugo was only three weeks old and needed intensive foster care.

Soon Hugo became a foster failure. He was simply too precious to let go of. Claudia adopted him.

His baby picture is displayed in the shop. It's easy to see why she fell in love.

Hugo has an incredible joy for life. He energizes the space around him, people smile and live in the moment. He has that incredible gift of being fully present. How wonderful that Hugo and his friends inspire us to take life by the leash and live it to the fullest!

Ari and Monkey©

The Barking Cat

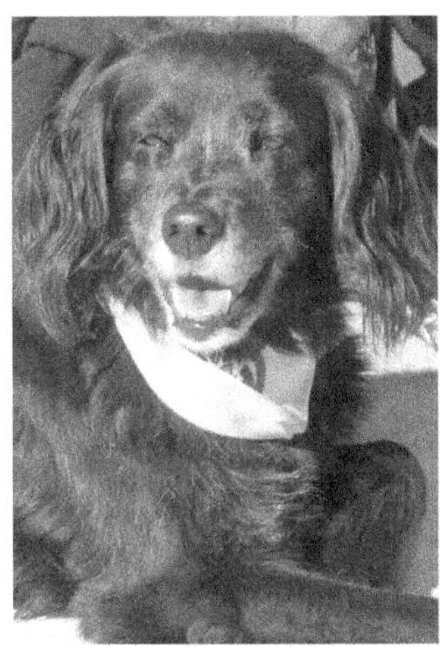

Maggie©

Meet Maggie the friendly greeter at The Barking Cat in Park City, Utah.

Maggie takes her self-appointed job very seriously. While there are many crucial things for her to help with around the store, there is nothing more important than giving each visitor a ladylike sniff, and a happy, welcoming wag.

Even if she is on one of her nap breaks, she gets up to greet visitors at the door right away. She sees her semi-retired, part-time schedule as no excuse to shirk duty.

Maggie will gladly accompany you to select a premium dog or cat food, or wellness supplements from Vitality Science. She loves to point out fun toys, collars and leashes by Wolfgang Man/Beast, or Cycle Dog.

She is always happy to help out at the Barkery, where all the nummy custom cakes and cookies are kept. If someone comes to the door while you are shopping, however, Maggie will politely excuse herself to greet the newcomer.

Maggie is a 14-year old Cocker Spaniel/Retriever mix with sparkling, good-humored eyes, a touch of gray around her muzzle, and her notorious toes that many say resemble the feet of The Grinch.

She was found wandering around the streets of Brigham City. She had been in the shelter long enough to be on their euthanasia list. Maggie was pulled from the shelter just in time by 4Paws Rescue. Sweet Maggie was then adopted at a big local adoption event.

At home, Maggie loves her Kong Frog and Squeakers, and she adores walks with her mom, Coleta Swenson.

Nothing makes a dog more content than having a job. Maggie excels at her chosen profession. Those of us fortunate enough to meet her, are gladdened by her warmth and gentleness.

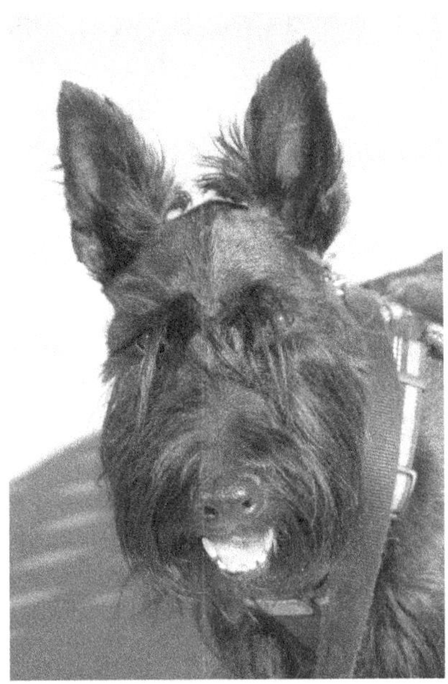

Dunkan©

Meet Dunkan, The Barking Cat's Scottish Terrier. He has a very important role at The Barking Cat. He is the mascot for the entire operation.

You will see lots of Scottie inspired merchandise and art in the store, all depicting the handsome face and joyful personality of a Scottish Terrier.

When Dunkan isn't working, he loves to travel with his mom, Merridee Hansen Farr Caruso, and then travel some more. He is always up for adventure.

At home, he is more of a couch potato, taking it easy & resting up until the next adventure begins.

Like many Park City residents, winter is Dunkan's favorite time of year. He loves to romp in the snow.

Dunkan is also a great watch dog! He watches for squirrels year-round.

Dunkan keeps a close eye on the Barkery. His nose knows that there are lots of luscious treats there. However, the real path to his heart is his favorite treat, Sam's Yams. Dunkan will do nearly *anything* for a Sam's Yam.

He takes this watch dog duty equally as seriously. He is vigilant and on-task.

In true Scottie fashion, Dunkan brings cheer and an upbeat energy with him everywhere he goes with his many chatterbox comments and super-fast wagging tail. His bright eyes reveal that he is a true comedian and adventurer!

Bridges to Better Living: How Animals Help Us Live Better Lives

Pearlie: My Service Dog ©

Far beyond enjoying the company of our companion animals, there is a healing connection that runs deep. Creatures from the animal kingdom have been helping humans heal for centuries, from the humble leech to the high-spirited horse.

"During the nineteenth century, the famous British nurse and author, Florence Nightingale, strongly advocated for the health benefits derived from animal companionship, and in her book Notes on Nursing (1860), she observed that small pet animals can help heal the sick."

Some companion animals are able to bridge the widest communication gaps to warn us of diseases like cancer, hypoglycemia, hyperglycemia, or impending seizures. They can help to ease our depression, stress, or anxiety. They can help to alleviate, and navigate, the symptoms of Post-traumatic Stress Disorder (PTSD).

These amazing companions can retrieve medication bottles or inhalers, or remind humans that it is time to take medications. They can provide deep-pressure therapy to help regulate the nervous system and help their human return to a state of calm embodiment.

They can help the hearing impaired know when the phone is ringing, when someone is at the door, or when an alarm goes off.

Others lead the sight impaired through their days, helping them cross busy intersections, use public transit, and navigate life's numerous complexities. They can give non-verbal autistic children a voice.

These special animals are bridges to human healing.

There are several types of Animal-Assisted Therapy:

(a) Service Dogs (and some miniature horses), who have public access rights, and must be task-trained to perform a task for a disabled individual.

(b) Emotional Support Animals: provide *general* emotional support and comfort by their presence and companionship with a person, but are not task-trained, and who do *not* have public access rights. An ESA does not have to be a dog (check ADA.gov for current regulations, and for special circumstances like housing access rights; it's a very narrow definition)

(c) Facility Animals: live in a facility and provide friendship to the facility's residents, not just one resident. They do *not* have public access rights.

(d) Therapy Animals: provide visits to people in facilities like hospitals and nursing homes. These animals live with their own humans, separate from the facility, have undergone extensive training to provide therapeutic visits, and do *not* have public access rights. Specially trained therapy dogs may even sit with children when they must testify in court. The dogs provide comfort and safety to these courageous children. Therapy dogs may also be found tending to first responders at a fire station or police station, helping to provide stress relief to community heroes.

We will be looking at some of the many aspects of Animal-Assisted Therapy and discover the answers to important questions along the way.

Bridges to Better Living: Service Dogs

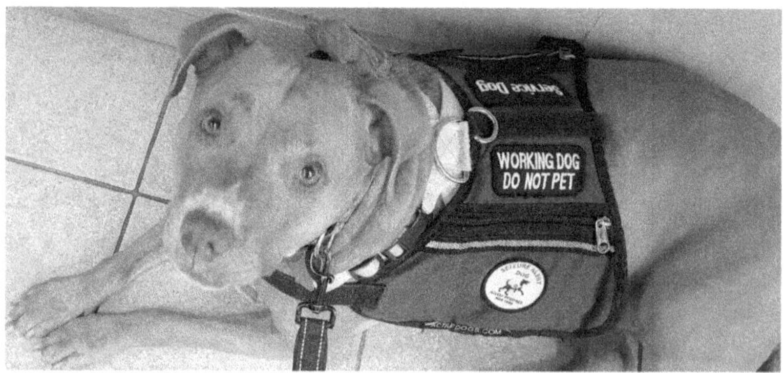

Pearlie: My Service Dog©

Service Dogs are in a class of their own. The United States Department of Justice defines Service Animals as "Dogs that have been trained to do work or perform tasks for people with disabilities."

Only dogs, and certain miniature horses, can be service animals.

Examples of such work or tasks include guiding people who are blind, alerting people who are hearing-impaired, pulling a wheelchair, alerting and protecting a person who is having a seizure, reminding a person to take prescribed medications, calming a person with PTSD (Post Traumatic Stress Disorder), waking a person from night terror episodes, alerting to changes in heart rate or blood pressure, or performing other duties for a variety of disabilities, as needed.

"The work or task a dog has been trained to provide as a Service Dog must be directly related to the person's disability. Dogs whose sole function is to provide comfort or emotional support do not qualify as service animals under the ADA (Americans with Disabilities Act)."

Service animals are working animals, not pets. As such, they are the ultimate companion animal.

Service Animals have public access rights that Therapy Animals, Emotional Support Animals, Facility Animals and pets do not.

Government offices and facilities, businesses and nonprofit organizations that serve the public must allow service animals to accompany people with disabilities in "all areas of the facility where the public is normally allowed to go," according to ADA.gov.

This access also applies to hospitals (with the exception of perhaps burn units and sterile operating rooms), taxis, shuttles, hotels, restaurants, grocery and department stores, medical offices, theaters, parks, zoos and health clubs, for example.

Service animals must be under the handler's control, and must be housebroken.

If it is unclear what service a dog (or miniature horse) performs, staff at a business may ask only these two questions of the handler:

1) Is the animal required due to a disability?

2) What tasks has the animal been trained to perform?

No other questions about the individual's disability, or the dog, are permitted. (See ADA.gov)

"Staff cannot ask about the person's disability, require medical documentation, require a special identification card or training documentation for the dog, or ask that the dog demonstrate its ability to perform the work or task," according to ADA.gov.

Fear of dogs, or allergies, are not valid reasons for denying service or entry to a person with a service animal.

Disabled people who are accompanied by their service animal cannot be discriminated against, isolated, treated less favorably than any other patron, or required to pay extra fees because they have a service dog.

"Violators of the ADA can be required to pay money damages and penalties," according to the ADA website.

When you see a service dog in public, remember that the dog is hard at work, performing duties and tasks for their handler.

Consider them equal to medical equipment. For example, you wouldn't ask to pet a person's walker or give their wheelchair a treat! The same holds true for a service dog.

DISTRACTION = DANGER

It is CRITICAL that you do NOT DISTRACT a service dog. Leave them alone.

Do not disturb their handler, who is likely using every last bit of energy they have to simply complete a task that might be easy for you.

Service dogs are highly tuned into their humans. They are trained to notice the subtlest of movements, scents and behaviors of their disabled person. Do not interrupt them.

NO TOUCH ~ NO TALK ~ NO EYE-CONTACT

IGNORE them, unless their human asks for help.

This is what a service dog needs from you in order to function at the intense level that their disabled human needs.

Do you want to make a service dog and their handler very happy? When you see them, ignore them, smile to yourself from afar, in gratitude for what these miraculous animals can do, and teach children that the best way they can help a service dog is by leaving them alone, so that they can do their job.

Praise children for being so kind and helpful, and please give them our thanks.

The most generous and gracious thing you can do for a service dog and handler team, is to allow them to go about their day, working together, bridging the gap between disability and successful daily living.

Bridges to Better Living: Emotional Support Animals

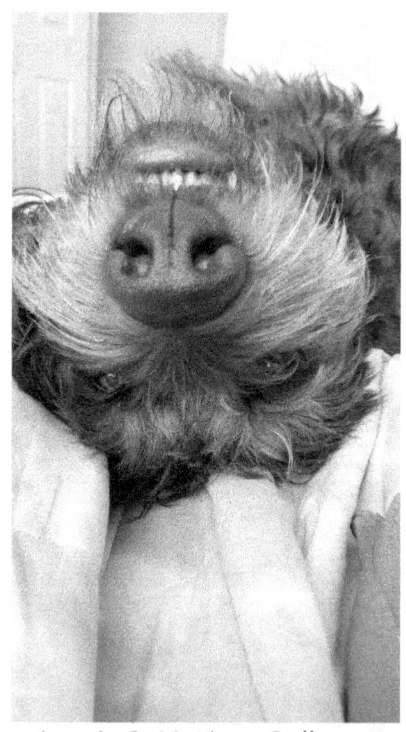

Auggie © Mariesa Galloway

In this chapter, we will continue to explore Animal-Assisted Therapy by considering the ways that Emotional Support Animals (ESAs) help humans to cope, and to heal.

Emotional Support Animals are of great benefit to human beings with debilitating emotional conditions. They provide comfort and consistent companionship that can help mitigate emotional and psychiatric symptoms.

For example, the mere presence of an emotional support animal may help to lessen the severity, or frequency, of panic attacks by helping to reduce stress and provide a calming effect.

They can help improve mood and emotional stability by the resulting increase of neurotransmitters in the human brain that are associated with a sense of overall well-being and happiness.

ESAs are wonderful at reducing loneliness and its harmful effects. They may help provide a sense of security and safety.

The care and daily routine needed by emotional support animals can be of tremendous help for people with depression or anxiety.

And the ESA's need for fresh air and exercise can help to encourage social interactions for their humans as well. Daily walks, going to the park, and interactions with other humans with pets all help to make socializing a bit easier and more enjoyable.

However, ESAs differ from Service Dogs, according to the Americans with Disabilities Act (ada.gov), including public access rights.

Let's compare:

- ESAs provide *general* emotional support and comfort by their presence and companionship with a person. ESAs are *not* task-trained.

- Service Dogs are task-trained to perform *specific* duties for their disabled handler, to help mitigate specific conditions and needs related to their handler's disability.

- ESAs can be species other than dogs.

- Service Animals are dogs, and in limited cases, miniature horses.

- ESAs cannot accompany their handlers inside public places like stores, restaurants, hospitals, hotels, libraries and the workplace.

- Service Dogs are allowed broad access to nearly *all* places that the public goes, with very few exceptions.

- ESAs *may* be allowed on aircraft but are *not guaranteed* access. Always contact the airline well ahead of time to get specific details about their regulations. Airlines may now treat ESAs as pets and therefore, charge a pet fee, place restrictions on species, size or breed, and limit the number of animals transported per flight.

- "Under the Air Carrier Access Act (ACAA) a service animal means a dog, regardless of breed or type, that is individually trained to do work or perform tasks for the benefit of a qualified individual with a disability, including a physical, sensory, psychiatric, intellectual, or other mental disability.

  - "Animal species other than dogs, emotional support animals, comfort animals, companionship animals, and service animals in training are not service animals."

Emotional Support Animals are remarkable and contribute so much to their human's well-being by their presence alone. Presence, and love, are their gifts of help and healing.

Bridges to Better Living: Animal-Assistance in Counseling & Therapy

Animal-assisted therapy can play a remarkable role when utilized in the counseling and therapy process.

For therapy to be most effective, practitioners seek ways to build trust and increase an individual's commitment to treatment.

Animal-Assisted Therapy (AAT) can help "enhance and expedite this stage," according to Minatrea & Wesley (2008), "The group using AAT appears more attached to the counseling process, places a higher value on the experience, and exhibits less stress during the process."

Individuals with Alzheimer's often have a combination of cognitive and mood disorders. "The presence of a therapy animal acts as an affective and emotional stimulus on patients and improves mood," according to Menna, Santaniello, Gerardi, et. Al. (2016).

According to Menna, L.F., Santaniello, A., Gerardi, F., Di Maggio, A., & Milan, G. (2016), "A dog understands non-verbal language and can function as a sounding board, acting as a stimulus as a result."

AAT intervention for those with Alzheimer's dementia may include stimulation of a memory about their own pets, structured play with the dog, caring for the animal by brushing, petting or giving treats.

Language skills can be practiced by storytelling, or by giving the dog a command and waiting for the performance of it.

AAT is also helpful in individual counseling for children who have been sexually abused. "The child may see the animal as a model, mirror or teacher. Because the animal is nonjudgmental, it can enhance the child's sense of self-esteem and promote the expression of feelings," according to Elizabeth Reichert, LCSW, Ph.D (1998). "Children often project their feelings about themselves onto the animal, which gives love, does not talk back or argue, and provides a continuous nonjudgmental relationship."

A child may also feel more comfortable relating the details of abuse to an animal; the child may be less intimidated as compared to verbally or otherwise describing the experience(s) to an adult.

This type of interaction gives the therapist the opportunity to learn about the child's situation by observing all of the non-verbal cues given, such as tone of voice, posture, and gestures.

The presence of an animal may also help the child feel strong and safe.

Anxiety is reduced. They are reassured that their voice matters because the animal is eager to listen.

Reichert concludes, "Animal-assisted therapy is an adjunct to play therapy. The animal serves as a bridge between the social worker and the child."

Another type of AAT, Hippo-therapy, or therapeutic horseback riding, has been found to be of benefit both physically and emotionally.

"Hippo-therapy literally means physical, occupational and speech therapy using the horse as a tool to address impairments, functional limitations, cognitive delays and disabilities with muscular dysfunction," according to Kelly, S. (2015). "The clients learn by participating in activities using the horse, processing feelings, behaviors, and patterns that result from that particular exercise."

What an incredible gift animals are in our lives! They help humans heal in so many ways. They deserve our very best stewardship and care.

Love for Their Lifetime

Toko©

Animal shelters and rescue organizations reported increased adoptions of companion animals during the Covid-19 pandemic. News reports showed empty kennels. During that period of social distancing, shelter-in-place orders, and isolation from other people, humans sought the comfort and friendship of companion animals to fill the void.

Adopting a pet requires us to not only meet their immediate needs. We must be diligent in taking great care of ourselves, so that we are healthy, able and available to care for and enjoy life with our animal companions.

Imagine what might happen to our companion animals if we become gravely ill and hospitalized. What are their needs? Who will meet those needs? It is important to have a backup plan for their care, and to share that plan with those who agree to take on the responsibility.

Please be sure to set aside funds for their ongoing care. So many beloved pets find themselves stranded when their human becomes too ill to return home, or passes away.

We recently adopted a Yorkshire Terrier. We weren't planning to adopt another dog, but the previous owner, our next door neighbor, lost a lifelong health battle. He didn't want to leave his little buddy. They loved each other very much.

It was heartbreaking to see such anguish and grief; the little pup's brown eyes brimmed with tears, his posture was slumped. He wouldn't walk; he crawled to me when we picked him up.

Our formerly happy, vivacious neighbor-pup was devastated and broken.

We could not fathom him being forced to live in an entirely new, and perhaps uncomfortable, environment. We could not leave his wellbeing to chance.

He had urgent and costly health problems that needed immediate medical attention. But we could not, would not, turn away from him.

We will never let him down.

When his "Papa's" human daughter asked us to adopt him, we said, "Yes." And meant it. He will live out his entire life with us loving him.

A few weeks after we adopted our Yorkie, Toko, our family was devastated.

My sister's amazing, happy, giant pup was diagnosed with cancer, had a kidney removed and was given a poor prognosis. My sister was faced with massive veterinary bills and the fear of losing her very good boy.

There was no wavering, however, in her decision to do whatever needed to be done to give him the best possible chance of surviving and thriving. Fortunately, a home refinance was possible to provide the funds for his surgery and chemotherapy.

He did well for a long while, spreading joy everywhere to everyone he met. My sister refused to quit on him. And he refused to quit too.

Then another tragedy hit. My service dog, Pearlie, received a completely unexpected and devastating diagnosis. Osteosarcoma. The vet sent us home with just two weeks of pain pills for her - he offered us no hope. We were crushed.

We relied on our faith and a greater power. I needed hope. She was ever-happy, with a strong, unbelievably strong, appetite for life. She survived nearly a year beyond those two weeks that the veterinarian gave us.

Just four years since Pearlie's diagnosis, the latest research from the College of Veterinary Medicine & Biomedical Sciences in Fort Collins, Colorado, shows that treatment is now possible for osteosarcoma.

There is now hope. It didn't arrive quick enough for her, but there is hope for others. Their cancer research also benefits humans, through cooperative studies and research. Gains are being made for dogs, humans, and other animals.

Pearlie's illness brought changes to our household. My kind husband was as committed as I was to make sure we met her needs.

We set a good, supportive mattress on the floor for her so that she would not injure herself getting on or off the bed. We bought a ramp to help her in and out of the car. We added firm cushions to the car to make the ride more comfortable.

We were not about to deprive her of anything she loved, including car rides. With the additional height, her new "little brother" could see out the window better - which he loved. I sewed new seat belt tethers to work with the new cushion setup.

My point is that when we bring a companion animal into our lives, it is a forever commitment. It is not just until we decide to do something else, or move somewhere else, or the family dynamics change. Their lives are our responsibility - and our profound joy.

I prayed and cried my way through many nights, when Pearlie appeared to be declining and we wondered if the end was near. She surprised us over and over, by getting up in the morning, determined to have a joyful day despite it all.

Our days were scheduled around doggy meals and medication times.

We counted every day as joy that we had with her. It was a tremendous honor and privilege to give her another bath, another cuddle, another ride in her wagon, and another belly rub.

Adoption of a companion animal is an act of *forever* love and sacrifice.

UPDATE: The end of the Covid-19 pandemic did not end well for thousands of animals who thought they'd found their forever homes.

It is now 2025 and shelters and rescues are again overflowing.

As people returned to the office, they returned pets to shelters, instead of working out ways to meet the needs of those dear animals. There are dog walkers, daycares, pet sitters who will come in to attend to fur-babies midday for little expense.

Our precious animal companions *must* be given top priority. They give us their *everything*.

They want nothing more than to be with us, even if we have to leave for a few hours a day to go to the office. They would so much prefer that, than languishing in an animal shelter and having their world upended.

Our companion animals comfort us when we are in need. We must not let them down. They are worth it. And they are counting on us to keep our promises.

Woof Notes: Training Saves Lives

Ripple & Toko at Training© Thanks, Overwatch-K9!

Animal shelters are filled beyond capacity. A huge number of the dogs who are surrendered by their owners, are adolescent dogs (appx. 8-months to 2-years old). The same people who adopted adorable little puppies give up on them at one of the most crucial points in a dog's life.

Canine teenagers struggle with many of the same difficulties as human teenagers. Their bodies grow faster than their brains. They seem to forget manners and behaviors that they learned easily as youngsters. They bump into boundaries. They get confused by the inconsistent, mixed messages that humans send them. And they do it all while their hormones are changing, their bodies and minds are changing, and their family members' lives are ever-changing too.

What do adolescent dogs need? The same thing human teenagers need: love, consistency, healthy boundaries, kind reminders of expected manners and behaviors, and help navigating their ever-changing *everything*.

Adolescent dogs may have setbacks that humans misinterpret as the dog being naughty, rebellious, or unmanageable. They may regress in some of their training, or struggle due to a lack of training altogether. Inconsistent, confusing messages from humans get even more confusing with hormones in the mix.

Empathy from us, their human companions, goes a long way toward helping our beloved pups through adolescence. We may do well to reminisce. Did we have any struggles as teenagers? What helped us get through that time in our lives?

We all see adoptable dogs as we scroll through our social media feeds. Dog after dog after dog. As we read through their physical descriptions, and information about their personalities, we also often read why their "family" surrendered them. Often, their only "sin" is being a teenager.

The failing is not on the canine. The failing is human caused.

When dogs are dropped off at the shelter, they are so confused. They do not understand why they are there. They wonder when their humans will return. Stress takes such a toll on them, just as stress is damaging to us.

One thing can save the health, both physical and mental, of adolescent dogs, and it can also save their lives.

TRAINING! That's right, training!

The solution to assist dogs who accidentally knock kids over, or dogs who bark, or dogs who pull on the leash, or dogs who have accidents in the house, or dogs who chew on walls or furniture, or dogs who are reactive, or chase anything with wheels, is TRAINING!

Dogs are putty in our hands. **They LOVE to learn. They LOVE to please us.** They live in the moment and enjoy life immensely.

All of their frustrations that may lead to behaviors that we find undesirable can be alleviated with a few things. First, dogs love to have a job. Second, they need an outlet. And third, they *love* quality time with their humans.

Training makes all of that possible!

Dogs can learn at every age. Just a few minutes of consistent training each day can improve life for you and your dog. Training can also keep dogs out of animal shelters. And training can help dogs get adopted into their forever homes.

Local professional trainers spend many volunteer hours at animal shelters, working with dogs to improve their behaviors, so that they have a better chance of getting adopted. Much of that training is simple: loose-leash walking, sit, down, place, and recall, for example. Teaching the dogs in our families those basic skills make our shared lives more enjoyable, and deepens the human-canine bond.

When you get a new dog in your family, sign them up for training classes with a reputable, professional trainer right away. No matter the age of the dog. Go through several series of classes, attend socialization groups, and never stop learning with your dog.

For those with adolescent dogs, keep going to training, keep practicing what you and your dog learn. **Training should always be fun and consistent**.

The canine brain matures at about two years of age. If you meet their needs, and give them that time to mature, you will have an amazing canine companion. And they'll have their forever home.

Woof Notes: I Think I Like This Little Dog

Ripple: My Service Dog©

To say I think I like this little guy is an understatement. I *love* everything about him. Yes, even the wild, comedic, zoomies-to-the-moon-and-back ways about him.

It all starts with his DNA, which we had tested immediately after we brought his little-itty-bitty-Pitti-self into his new forever home. We expected the results to be a Pitti mix, but nope, to our surprise, he is a 100% American Pit Bull Terrier (APBT).

Did we run for the hills in fear? Ha! No way! From our experience living with and loving Pitties, we know the rumors spread by the media in their efforts to frighten the public for ratings, are simply sensationalism.

My first service dog was a Rottweiler. The second a Pit Bull, and now, Ripple. All have been excellent, gentle, sensitive, partners.

Terrible events happen, of course. *All* dogs with teeth may bite if terrorized, teased, provoked or cruelly trained to do so. Terriers, whether Yorkie, Airedale, Bedlington, Jack Russell, Staffordshire, or Pit Bull, have tenacious, energetic, drives.

Pitties are strong dogs. When humans use those traits for evil, by torturing those dogs to train them (in the most ghastly, horrific, ways) to injure others, whether human or canine, the result is un-speakable suffering. The tortured dogs suffer endlessly because they are forced to do what their kind hearts would *never* do on their own.

However, the vast majority of Pit Bulls are gentle, energetic (in short stints – they do require their beauty sleep and lots of it), cuddly, playful and loyal dogs. They have a comedic sense of humor and love to please their humans.

They are stunning in appearance; a perfect blend of strength cloaked in velvet. Our Ripple has the most gorgeous brindle coat I have ever seen. People stop us all the time to comment on his brindle-beauty.

He also has ooey-gooey-chocolatey eyes, with a serious knack for throwing us the side-eye whenever he thinks we have lost our minds, which is often. He is hilarious. His ears and muzzle are pure velvet to the touch.

Ripple is an epic prancer, a one-dog prancing parade at every opportunity! Each morning, upon waking, he grabs the nearest toy or shoe (gently, of course, never destructive) and leads the good morning parade, in full high-stepping prance mode, checking behind him to make sure my husband is following him to the living room to greet me and our Yorkie, Toko. The fact that no one else is prancing with such joie de vivre does nothing to dampen his enthusiasm.

Ripple never meets a stranger. He believes with all his heart that everyone, no matter the species, is his new best friend. His buddies include bumble bees, ducks and ducklings, butterflies, hummingbirds, geese (from a distance, because they're spicy), dogs, humans, feral cats that spring up at him from the weeds along the ditch bank (also from a distance, due to their spiciness), and humans.

Now that he's an adult, his ability to discern human intentions and energy has improved, and he will assert aloofness when he deems it necessary. I appreciate that trait in each of my beloved service dogs. They've all had that innate, highly-tuned sense of situational awareness that make it possible for me to navigate the public with more confidence and sense of safety.

My friend, Mere Morckel, and her family, have been pet sitters for decades. She told me that the most well-behaved, jolliest, and easy dogs they've tended have all been Pitties. Of course, proper socialization, training, and love, make that possible. *All* dogs need that.

As for Ripple, his hilarious sense of humor, his comedic antics, his energy, head-tilts, zoomies, and love, were all key in helping me as I grieved the loss of my beloved Pearlie, so intensely. She was my ABPT, and service dog. I did not know how I could move forward without her.

I questioned if I could ever get another dog, due to knowing that I would eventually grieve their loss also. The thought was just too much for me to handle.

However, the day came when I thought, *"The BEST way to honor Pearlie, and all that she meant to me, is to ADOPT ANOTHER."*

We rescued Pearlie, literally, as her former owners were driving to dump her at the shelter. How could I possibly honor her more, than by saving another?

Ripple's Gotcha-Day © Rachel Horvat
Brighton

Within days of that decision, Ripple's little face popped up in my social media feed. I knew that he was the one. It wasn't just that he was adorable – it was that I could FEEL his presence by my side.

I flooded the rescue organization with phone calls, texts, and emails from every contact source I could find. His foster mama was hiking that day, but got back to me right when she returned home.

I met him as soon as possible. I waited in her yard as she retrieved him from the house. He ran, full steam ahead, up a few stairs, across the lawn, onto my lap and into my arms. What joy!

I already knew he was my new companion before I got there. But his foster mama was stunned: he had avoided all other humans who had come to meet him.

She saw him run to me, wriggle and wiggle, and run back and forth across my lap, and she too had no doubt we were meant to be.

Deep in my soul, I believe that God always provides just the right dog, at just the right time. He has proved that over and over. It makes me more aware. It makes me wonder what I am to learn from loving each dog He sends. It makes me immensely grateful for each one.

I LOVE this little dog. All 70-pounds of him.

Ripple ©

Woof Notes: Caution! Toxins!

Let's look at some common environmental toxins that impact our companion animals. As they nuzzle, snuggle and snuffle their way through life, they are often exposed to toxins at higher concentrations than humans are, simply because they are closer to the ground.

They also have fewer options since they did not choose their environment and can do little to influence a change. The responsibility is ours. We are the stewards of their lives, health and happiness.

Mammals can be injured by toxins that enter their bodies in four main ways: through the skin, which is the largest organ, through inhalation, through membranes, or through ingestion.

The list of toxins is daunting.

Indoors, they may be damaged by mold, certain essential oils, fragrances, detergents, fabric softeners, enzymatic cleaners, food items, deodorizers, toothpaste, mouthwash, Firestarter logs, hand sanitizer, floor cleaners, cleaning products (including wipes), cosmetics, potpourri, pesticides (including flea & tick prevention products), chemicals in new carpet, plastic dishes and toys, chemically saturated rawhide chews, lead, asbestos, drug residue, oven-cleaning fumes, remodeling detritus, second-hand smoke, and household plants.

Outdoor dangers include mold, fungi, protozoa, antifreeze, ice melting products, trash, traps, insecticides, herbicides, fertilizers, pesticides, poisons, algae, mushrooms and many of the same items that are included in the list of indoor dangers.

We must *always* watch out to be sure our companion animals do not ingest the *deadly* sweetener, xylitol, also known as birch sugar, in any of its many forms. It can be found in everything from chewing gum to peanut butter. Read labels carefully to protect your fur baby.

This partial list is exhausting, but not exhaustive.

What can we do to protect our companions from the gauntlet of deadly toxins?

Do your research and be vigilant. Pay specific attention to the environments you share. Look at your home and yard through their eyes. Dust and vacuum often. Avoid toxic cleaning solutions, especially sprays and any cleaner that their paws will touch.

Mop with a steam cleaner that requires no chemicals or detergent. Change your furnace filter frequently, use a high-quality filter that removes dander and allergens. Use a white vinegar solution for disinfecting surfaces and even as a fabric softener, especially for pet bedding.

Throw away plastic pet dishes and replace them with stainless steel or ceramic (be careful to make sure the paint contains no lead). Toss out toxic toys and treats. Use organic solutions in the yard, avoid chemicals as much as possible.

Just like humans, even if our companion animals exhibit no neg-ative effects, or allergic symptoms, from contact with toxins, their bodies still have to fight them off to be healthy.

Let's make it as easy on them as we can. They love and protect us, let's do our part for them.

Woof Notes: Prepare to Evacuate!

Companion animals and livestock are family members. If our lives are in danger, their lives are in danger too! We must always be diligent, not only in the care of our human families and ourselves, but in the care of our animal companions.

The fires in Utah's mountain ranges and foothills each year are examples of tragedies in the making. They may not be as large in scale as hurricanes along coastal areas, but can be devastating in a quick period of time, like the recent wildfires in the Los Angeles area.

What can we do to prepare for a natural, or man-made, disaster?

Prepare in advance, as much as possible. If you need to vacate, don't wait. Leave as early as you can, to avoid traffic jams, and reach pet-friendly accommodations ahead of the crowd. Practice multiple escape routes, know where you can stay, such as pet-friendly shelters, hotels, campgrounds or with friends or family.

Think outside the box, be creative. Flee farther away to get reservations easier. Find a kennel that you are comfortable with, and be sure to have your pets spend some time there occasionally, so that they are comfortable too.

Keep vehicles licensed, insured, fueled up, and in good operating condition.

Teach your companion animals to come to you quickly when called, or to come to a whistle that can be heard over the sound of loud alarms. Crate train dogs and cats, muzzle train dogs (even if you don't think they need it), because some shelters require that. Write your contact information and your animal's name in permanent marker on their crate.

MICROCHIP your pets - and ***REGISTER* THE MICROCHIP!** Keep that information updated. Many times a month, I see posts on social media asking for help to locate a missing pet that is microchipped - but the microchip has never been registered!

Affix a pet alert sticker to a front window of your home, so that first responders know how many pets to look for, and the location of their crates in the house. Every second counts.

Some people choose to use a magic marker and write information on their animal's back or belly. Some have their veterinarian "tattoo" contact information and medical information on their animals.

Create a Bug-out Kit. Pack a tote with: seat belts, harnesses, spill-proof dishes, ID tags, veterinary records, pet insurance policy documents, a photo of you with your companion animal (to help prove ownership if you get separated), phone numbers of trusted friends/family, instructions on how to care for your fur babies, medications and dosing instructions, and enough food for several weeks (rotate food and medications every six-months).

Pack a pet first aid kit, litter box and litter, waste bags, paper towels, disinfectant, blankets and beds, toys and treats, veterinary-approved calming remedies, duct tape (to repair tote or crate if damaged), pet parents' worn unwashed shirts (in sealed plastic bags - to preserve scent) to use for bedding and comfort, grooming tools like brushes and combs, nail trimmer, pet wipes and hand sanitizer.

Install a combination key-box on your home. They are available at hardware stores. Give the combination to a trusted neighbor who is home most of the time. They may be able to take your pets with them to safety if you are not home.

Create a neighborhood buddy system to help with emergency situations and evacuations. Notify each other where you'll be staying during the evacuation.

If you have livestock, have a buddy system in place with community members who have trucks and trailers. Help each other get your livestock to safety. Just as with household animal companions, do not leave them to die.

Have ID on your livestock as normal practice in case they are caught in a sudden fire or flood with no time to evacuate. Keep photos and ownership records in a safe place - you may need to prove ownership after the emergency.

Identify pet-friendly shelters. Be aware of your options. If you don't have a pet-friendly shelter in your community, gather like-minded people and organize one.

Save lives, suffering and heartache by pulling pet-friendly resources together in **advance** of the next emergency.

Woof Notes: Summer Fun with Your Canine Companion

Georgia © Crystal Stonehocker

Summer is here! Opportunities abound for outings and adventures, and our canine companions will be eager to join us. With good planning and preparation, our dogs can be included in many safe summer events.

Before your dog joins you in outdoor events, it is crucial to understand your dog's health limitations, including but not limited to, stamina and summer temperature tolerance.

This information can be assessed from your knowledge of your companion dog's previous veterinarian visits. Also, veterinary clinics are more than happy to complete a short wellness visit and provide you with a written medical report plus any needed medications.

Heat, especially summer heat, can, in various situations, prove lethal to your dog. A good practice to follow is this: if the temperature feels "hot" to us, it is even hotter for our dogs.

Issues that can adversely affect our dogs while on outings may include their weight, matted fur that doesn't allow airflow, short snouts that decrease a dog's ability to breathe and to cool down by panting, short legs that keep their bodies close to the hot turf, dark colored and /or heavy fur that may absorb heat, and hot turf that will easily burn their foot pads.

Recently, Park County Search and Rescue from Colorado (pcsar. org) posted a plea for humans to assess their dogs' needs before setting out on an adventure. They said, "Your dog doesn't know how far 'too far' is. That's **your** job."

Just last week, this search and rescue group had been called out twice, each time to rescue a dog who had been run to utter exhaustion. (https://www.facebook.com/ParkcountySAR).

They recommend dog owners always have a Fido Pro Rescue Sling with them (fidoprotection.com) for assistance in carrying their dog to safety. A sturdy tote bag with the ends cut open, or a firewood carrier could also work for *short* distances. Even an almost weightless bedsheet can be stashed in a backpack; a useful home-made sling for your dog or your hiking companion!

Personally, I carry a Fido Pro Rescue Sling, or have my Pittie wear the harness version, the Fido Pro Panza Harness V2. Although it is not crash-tested (I wish it was) he can wear it as a harness/seatbelt restraint on the way to our adventure.

Then he can carry the gear that can easily be converted to a sling in case of an emergency or injury, so that I can carry him in a way that is doable for me, and would be the safest, most comfortable way for him.

Information to Remember:

- NEVER leave your dog in a car, even in the shade with the windows cracked

- Leave your dog at home if you can't guarantee their comfort and safety

- Avoid exercising your dog during hotter times of the day

- Hold the back of your hand to the pavement or concrete for seven seconds without moving. **If it is too hot for your skin, it *will* burn your dog's paws**

- Carry plenty of cool water for your dog and yourself; seek shade and take frequent breaks

Summer Activity Ideas:

- Set up a kiddie pool or sprinkler in the shade for your dog

- Play indoor scent games, puzzles, and agility; be creative and make it fun

- Provide your dog with frozen treats, stuffed Kong toys, or dog-safe ice cream

- Teach your dog some new tricks by playing training games

- Head for the mountains to enjoy cooler temperatures at higher elevations

- Relax on a shady lawn and let the world go by while your dog enjoys sniffing the breeze

Have a wonderful, fun-filled, safe summer. Enjoy it even more by including your Canine Companion!

Woof Notes: The Plight of Homeless Cats

The plight of homeless cats is heartbreaking. According to peta.org, "It is estimated that between 60 and 100 million homeless cats live in the U.S."

It is difficult, if not impossible, to comprehend a number so large.

We must realize that *each one* of these 100 million homeless cats represents a sentient being, a cat who has emotions, a unique personality, and needs that are emotional as well as physical.

Homeless cats struggle to survive. They lack the luxury of a consistent food source, clean water, and a safe living environment. Constantly on the lookout for food and for predators, their nervous systems are in continual fight-or-flight mode. They typically have a much shorter lifespan than domestic, tame cats.

Homeless cats are categorized into three sub-groups; homeless, wild, and feral. They often live tragic lives and deaths, seldom having the opportunity of dying because of "age-related" health issues. Automobile injuries, poisoning, fatal diseases including those they have not been vaccinated against, and death resulting from other animals are typical causes. Tragically, many die at the hands of cruel humans.

Their lives are most often void of human love, consistent nutrition, and medical care. They are starved of affection, safety, nutrition, water and shelter. They are forced to scrap, scrounge and fight to survive.

Why are there so many homeless kitties? The main contributor is rapid, uncontrolled breeding.

"A female cat can produce an average litter size of 5 kittens, three or four times per year-each year!" according to peta.org.

The uncontrolled population grows exponentially each year.

Cats also become homeless when humans abandon or relinquish them to shelters. Oftentimes, shelters are not equipped to care for these cats. Various states have differing rules and regulations as to the care of drop-offs. Many have adoption programs, TNR programs, and some simply euthanize when necessary. The types of euthanization practices are of grave concern for many states.

How can you help? First, spay and neuter your cats. Unwanted litters and unadopted kittens have a greater risk of becoming part of the homeless cat population.

Secondly, to help the already-feral cats in your community, check with local animal shelters to see if a Trap-Neuter-Return (TNR) program is available in your area. With TNR, cats are caught, spayed or neutered, immunized, and ear-clipped for identification of an altered, immunized cat. They also are given a Rabies vacci-nation, which is a law in most states. After TNR, cats are returned to their home-community. Helping to reduce the future number of homeless cats is a proactive way to help these cats survive.

Many TNR programs are equipped, with the support of local shel-ters and volunteers, to provide clean water, nutritious food, and adequate shelter. Cats who have adequate food, water and shelter do not have the severe survival issues as unattended cats.

Volunteering with your local animal shelter, or with a rescue or-ganization, is a good way to help homeless cats. Reach out to see what their needs are. Donations are always needed in order for them to provide veterinary care, food, dishes, litter, carriers, transportation and emergency care.

Foster if you are able. Each time a cat is able to leave the shelter to stay with a foster, an opening is created for another stray cat.

Adopt if you can. Every cat that is adopted makes a space with a shelter or a rescue to help another.

Share and help spread the word. Share listings from shelters and rescue organizations of cats that need homes. Even if you are not in a position to foster or adopt, please keep sharing to pass along their information to your contacts and to the community.

And always in your own way and community, spread the word for people to spay and neuter, and to *always* be kind to animals.

______

 https://www.webercountyutah.gov/Animal_Shelter/community-ty-feral-cat.php

Auggie: The Bestest Button & IT Expert

Auggie: The Button ©
Mariesa Galloway

Surprised. That was my reaction to the news that my sister was searching through rescue websites to find a Schnauzer. A Giant Schnauzer. The east bench bungalow she shares with her husband is small on square footage. I couldn't imagine fitting a dog larger than our Rottweiler into their living space.

"Good thing they have a big fenced yard. A puppy that size is going to need a lot of exercise," I thought.

lp To try to discourage her, or encourage her in a smaller-dog direction, would have been folly. Instead, I started to think of ways I might help to help ensure a successful adoption.

For months, my sister had been joining my dogs and I on walks and at the dog park. People would chat us up and ask my sister which dog was hers; my Rottweiler, Sadie, or my newly adopted Pit Bull puppy, Pearlie. "Neither, they are my sister's dogs. I just enjoy coming along with them," she'd say.

I should have seen the Giant Schnauzer coming.

The phone call soon came. "We are going to Southern Utah to get our Giant Schnauzer!" she squealed.

I was stunned. I couldn't believe how quickly she had found a pup of that breed.

"Are you online? I'll send you the pictures. I am so excited!"

The heart wants what the heart wants.

Wondering if she was really ready, I took a deep breath and re-minded myself what a beautiful, loving and capable person my sister is. I knew her heart was ready, and the details would be handled step by step.

A long day passed as she planned her trip. She hardly slept that night.

In the morning, another call came. "They found the dog we were going to meet dead in the yard this morning. They think it might have been a seizure," she said.

"Oh no, I am so sorry, Sis." I worried what this new grief might manifest as in her life. No one likes to see their loved ones hurting.

Her heart was broken, but her spirit was undeterred.

A few days later I answered my sister's call. She could hardly contain herself. "I found him! I found our dog. He's the one, I know it. I can't get to him quick enough!"

The heart knows what the heart knows.

I prayed that this pup would be healthy and that her heart would not be broken again.

"Tell me more about him. Do you have any pictures?" I asked.

"He is so cute!"

I knew she was deeply in love with him already; sight-unseen.

"Why is he up for adoption? Just curious," I asked.

"His family got him as a puppy and they can't keep him because they said he keeps knocking their kids over. He is with the Adopt Me Society rescue group now. He is perfect!"

Soon, Auggie (formerly known as Maximus) was adopted into our family pack. My aging Sadie thought he was pretty fun and Pearlie (formerly known as Princess) fell madly in love with him, and he with her. I've never seen two dogs enjoy spending time together as much as Auggie and Pearlie. They share an epic, though spayed and neutered, romance.

With exercise, clear boundaries, patience, high-quality food and lots of love, Auggie has become a very handsome gentleman. One of his favorite friends is our 6-year old niece. We don't worry about Auggie with kids anymore, he is a gentle giant. He loves to stand tall and firm while kids lean on him, hug him and snuggle with him. He makes frequent trips to visit the children at Deamude Adventist Christian Academy (K-8), and loves to go camping with a local youth group, Pathfinders, that is full of children to love and play with.

As Auggie grows, he looked less and less like a Schnauzer. Out of curiosity, my sister sent in a DNA test to find out his roots. Auggie is part Black Labrador, part Golden Retriever, and part German Wirehair Pointer. And he is huge. His feet are much larger than the palm of my hand. We affectionately refer to him as our pony.

Auggie's loving, playful, compassionate heart is bigger than the whole of him. He has brought so much joy into our family; his new family. He was meant to be with us.

I feel foolish for thinking that the square footage of their home was too small. I know that the square footage of my sister's heart knows no bounds. I love that about her.

Auggie is a perfect fit.

Auggie: IT Expert and Bestest Bubba ©

*Jacque & Sadie at the Colorado National
Monument © Mariesa Galloway*

One Easier Path Through Grief

From the day we bring a new animal companion into our hearts and homes, we know that the day will likely come when we will have to say goodbye to them. That day always comes much too soon. They are so special, and such an integral part of our lives, of the very essence of us, that the grief can be overwhelming. I've said goodbye too many times, as has any animal lover.

Our family faced grief again, just a few weeks ago. I wondered how long I would be a mess, and to what degree. The previous loss had taken me about a year to come to grips with. I prepared myself for another year's sentence.

However, mercifully, this time was different.

Two years ago, when our 3-legged miracle Rotti, Lexi, passed away, a family member offered help to me, but I didn't invite her into my pain. I felt it would be too excruciating to open that wound, even though I knew she could help. I just couldn't go there.

However, three weeks ago, when our sweet Sadie passed away, I had to cry out for help. I wasn't coping. I was desperate to numb the pain, even just a tiny bit, in order to function. My grief was raw, bare, and deep.

Mom rushed over.

For years, my mom has been studying the science of N.L.P., Neuro-Linguistic Programming. She has earned her Master Practitioner's certificate and is excellent at her work. I'm glad I finally allowed her to use the process with me that she had written specifically to help me heal two years prior. I regret waiting those two years.

We went into a quiet room in my home, she had me choose a way to sit or lay that felt most comfortable and relaxed, and she gently guided my mind through the written, healing process. N.L.P. is different from hypnosis because you remain fully alert, fully conscious, fully in control. You simply allow your mind to respond to the process script and language in a way that is the most appropriate for your belief system, and that is most healing to you.

We spent about 20-30 minutes together, and then she left me alone to be still and relax. I was at peace, knowing I had done the very best for Sadie that I could. She lived a very happy life. I was able to focus on the multitude of happy memories that we shared with her, instead of the difficulties of her last day. I was able to rest.

In the weeks that have followed, I've had a couple of hard cries. I'm okay with that. It's healthy to have emotions and to grieve. However, I have also been able to move forward, to enjoy memories and photos of her without plunging into the dark abyss of depression, like I have done following the loss of beloved pets prior.

My brief experience with just one N.L.P. process has made such an incredible difference. I am grateful that my mom developed the process specifically for those of us experiencing grief. I'm also grateful for her patience and gentle nudging, reminding me that she had developed a way for this independent daughter to experience life's losses in a gentler way.

Dear Reader, my hope, is that when you suffer a loss, you will reach out for help in whatever modality is most helpful for you. Remember that there is an easier way, a gentler way, a truly healing way, to walk through the grief, and reach the point more quickly, where you can cherish your joyous memories, rather than get stuck in the sadness of painful loss. Help is available. If you are in crisis, call 988 immediately to speak with someone who can help. Or call 911 if you are in danger of physical harm.

Our wonderful animal companions are gifts to us the day they arrive in our lives. Their memories are cherished gifts to carry us forward, while bringing a smile to our lips. The healing I received through the N.L.P. process ensures smiles unlimited whenever I think of Sadie.

FICTION

"Reading fiction is important. It is a vital means of imagining a life other than our own, which in turn **makes us more *empathetic* beings**." ~ Ann Patchett

Fiction, like parables, makes concepts real, relatable, understandable, easily sharable, and memorable. Our hearts and minds are opened, and we are able to become deeply connected to one another through *empathy*.

Our world *needs* more empathy.

At Heart

The holidays loomed lonely at the care center, despite the festive decor and the ever-lit fireplace in the foyer. The tinsel had been hung with care. The staff did their best for the residents, but long shifts and short staffing didn't allow for much.

Night shifts were tough. The sadness of some residents could never be comforted. All anticipated the light of day, in hopes of lighter hearts.

Adele, the registered nurse, pushed her medication cart down the hall, waking up residents to give them their pills.

Quiet cooing spilled into the hall from Mr. Blaine's room. "Oh, Angel, I've missed you so."

Adele was stunned. She had not heard him speak in months. *This shift is really getting to me..* She shook her head to clear her tired mind and continued her round.

"How did you find me?" asked Mr. Blaine. "No one knows I'm here."

Adele stopped, locked her cart and walked softly to his door. She leaned forward to listen. He spoke no more. But happy, content little sounds continued to float out of his room like fireflies in a dark sky.

Adele went back to work, convinced he must be talking in his sleep.

"Sorry to wake you, Mr. Blaine. I have your medication for you." She handed him a little cup with his pills in it and a sip of water. "Were you having a dream earlier?"

Mr. Blaine pointed at the notepad & pen on the bedside table. She handed them to him and noticed his hands. They were strong, proof of a life of hard work, yet gentle.

"I can't talk anymore," he wrote.

"That's what I thought too, but I'm pretty sure I heard you talking to someone a few minutes ago. Maybe these night shifts are playing tricks on me."

"I talk in my mind, but no matter how hard I try, I can't get the words out now." He tried hard to smile the best he could, though one side of his face still drooped from the stroke. "What did I say?"

She told him, word for word.

Confusion registered on his face. "I was dreaming about my favorite old mare. I named her Angel. She had a mind of her own, but she was so steady! When other people were around, she'd create a fuss, put on an ornery show. But back at the barn, she'd press her long, lithe neck across my chest. It was like a bear hug! She was something special!"

Writing about Angel tuckered him out. He drifted back to sleep.

Adele smiled and put the notepad and pen back on the table. As she tidied up to leave, a noise caused her to turn around. Mr. Blaine was tapping on the bed rail to get her attention. He pointed at the bedside table.

"Do you smell that?" he wrote. "It's that sweet scent of horse lather after a good day's work. That's what woke me earlier, when I thought I was dreamin' and you thought I was talkin'. I guess my guardian angel knew I needed a comforting memory tonight."

"I have my doubts, Mr. Blaine. I'm not one who believes in ghosts."

"Me either!" he wrote, "but I know God gave me a guardian angel. And one great horse."

As Adele turned out the lights, she paused in the doorway. *Huh. Horse lather.*

In another room, Rosie giggled. A smile spread across her face and a single tear escaped her hazel eyes. Her delicate hands patted the bedspread.

"Oh my, you are still as big as a pony! Jump up here, like you used to."

Adele listened to Rosie talk in her sleep. Rosie had told the staff many tales about the Great Dane she once rescued.

"He was all ears and legs for the first year. And paws! What huge paws! They were second only to the size of his appetite, which was dwarfed only by his love of snuggling!"

Adele could not imagine life with a beast that big, no matter how snuggly.

"Lay right here beside me. Warm me up. I'm always so cold since you had to leave me."

Adele hoped that Rosie's dream would warm her up. She was so lonesome, despite the many visitors she had each week. She always complained of being cold, even though the heat in her room was stifling to anyone who dared enter.

"Rosie, sorry to wake you, dear. I have your pills."

"Now you stay right where you are so I can take my pills. Keep your giant head , and the rest of you, under that table, or they'll see you and make you leave," whispered Rosie, though none too quietly.

"Who are you talking with?"

"Who, me? No one at all. Just a crazy old lady talking in her sleep." Rosie flashed her most convincing smile, hoping to be believed.

Adele smiled in her gentle way. "Is that so?"

"Yes. Probably dreaming," said Rosie, clearly trying to cover her story.

"Can I get you an extra blanket, one from the warmer?"

"Oh, dear, no! Are you crazy? I would roast!"

"Well, we sure don't want that! Are you feeling ill? Feverish or anything?" asked Adele, as she straightened Rosie's covers. She noticed they felt much warmer than expected.

"No, dear, this is the best I've felt since I got here. I've been given the gift of a very warm memory tonight."

"I'm so happy for you, Rosie. Goodnight."

"Night-night. Will you please turn down the heat on your way out?"

Adele reached for the thermostat. *I am losing what little is left of my mind!*

Adele turned her cart toward the pediatric unit. She adored the kids, though their need of long-term care broke her heart every day. The ventilators were the loudest sound on the floor. Most of the children were silent, except for the coughing fits that set off the ventilator alarms. The little ones with brain damage couldn't talk, laugh, or even cry. Adele believed that meant they needed her love all the more. The nurses and aides all felt that way.

Alarms began screeching three doors down. Adele sprinted to help.

Jordy's eyes were open. He was looking intensely at the chair near his bed. He had been injured in a near-drowning accident the year before. Now ten years old, he faced life with a brain injury; he hadn't spoken, or moved anything below his shoulders, since.

"Jordy, do your best to relax. I'm here to help. I'll get your tube cleared so you can breathe easier."

Jordy moved his head left and right. The alarms quieted.

"Jordy, you just moved your head! Was that on purpose?"

Jordy's eyes sparked then locked with hers.

The movement *was* intentional!

"I'm so happy for you! What fantastic progress! I'll be sure to let your care team know. You get some good rest and we will celebrate more in the morning."

Jordy moved his head again. Slower. Once left. Once right.

"Hey, Mister," she teased, "don't you be showing off all night now. You need your rest."

Adele resumed her walk to the next room. The alarms sounded again. She ran back to him.

"What is it, Jordy? Are you okay?" His eyes were focused on the chair again.

"Your mom will be back in the morning, I'm sure," she said.

One-sided conversations were tough. Adele was frequently on the guessing end.

Jordy shook his head. Then he tried to speak. The loud, shrill alarms sounded off again.

Adele leaned in close and focused hard. She couldn't understand what he wanted her to know. *This poor kid, trapped in his own head!* She kept working with him.

Soon, he was very direct. He looked at the box of gloves on the wall. Then the chair. Gloves. Chair. Repeat.

"Do you want something with the gloves, Jordy?"

Head left. Head right.

Adele pondered the possibilities. *What does he mean? I want to get this right.*

"Mittens?" she asked.

Jordy's eyes lit up.

"That's it! Jordy, you want mittens? Are you cold?"

His eyes said, "Um...duh. No." Then they went to the picture of his cat on the bulletin board. Mittens had passed away a few months before his accident.

"Oh, Jordy, of course," she said. "You miss Mittens."

Gloves. Chair. Then his eyes closed. Exhausted. But a slight smile remained.

Though Jordy had no way to tell Miss Adele, the memory of Mittens was so real. It was as though he could hear Mittens purr and feel her soft paws kneading his shoulders and chest. A memory so vivid, calming and treasured, that Jordy hoped it was powerful enough to bring speech back to his long-silent lips and motion back to his atrophied muscles.

During shift change at the nurse's station, Adele told her replacement, "It's been a strange shift. But it seems our Creator has been very busy with His healing hands here tonight."

"Merry Christmas, Adele", said Betsy, as she took their much-loved patients under her wing.

Adele smiled as she pulled her parka tight around her, bracing for the winter wind. *What a special Christmas Eve. One to remember.*

A Week In the Life of a Shelter Cat

"Mom, may I keep her? Please?"

Sandy squealed with joy when her mom nodded and said, "Yes."

"I'll take extra good care of her," Sandy promised.

The kitten shared in the excitement. She pranced back and forth, rubbing her silky fur on the front of the pen. "Hurry and open this door!" she thought, "Pet me, hold me."

At her new home, her humans bustled about, setting up a place for a litter box, and another for food and water bowls. They set up a toy box, filled with lots of fun toys. They kept her busy, feeding, petting and playing with her.

"Oh, what fun! I had no idea life could be so wonderful!" she thought that night as she drifted off to sleep in her new bed, snuggled up with her new little girl.

When she woke up the next morning, she was all alone in the great big house. Panic set in. "Where can I hide? I don't feel safe!"

Bam! Bam! Bam! A loud noise on the front door startled her. She climbed to the top of the living room curtains to hide. Bam! Bam! The door rattled again. She crouched down, making herself as small as possible, to watch the door from her place in the drapes until the scary noise went away.

"I like the way this feels on my toes," she thought, as she kneaded the fabric of the drapes. She raced down them, then up , then down, then up again. She was amazed at the way the fabric let her claws sink in to support her body weight. "I love this! This is the best thing my humans gave me!"

At last, her humans returned home. "What happened to my new drapes?" yelled the mother.

"I'd better hide!" she thought as she raced to the top again.

"That cat is out of here first thing tomorrow morning," said the mother. Sandy began to cry. "I'm sorry, dear, but your cat just destroyed my very expensive new drapes."

The next day, the kitten sat, shivering, in a cage in the animal shelter. "I don't understand this at all. I loved them so much and I tried to be a very good kitty."

Her cage was opened a few times each day by nice people who called her Sheba. They gave her food and water. They cleaned her litter box. She purred and pranced and rubbed on their hands to get them to love her and take her far away from the noisy shelter, to no avail.

Each day, she got a bit more used to the noise, but the loneliness was unbearable.

"Why did my humans throw me away? I hope they come back for me."

Each time the kennel door opened, she jumped up to see if it was her humans. But they never returned.

One by one, the other cats disappeared. Sometimes a family adopted them, other times a technician took them away and never brought them back. Fear hung heavy in the air. "What happens to them?"

Over and over she heard, "Can I keep this one, Mom & Dad?"

She was so happy for them. "At least they'll be free from here, even if it's only for a little while."

Every cage that was emptied was filled again with a new, scared, lonely kitty. "It's never-ending," she thought.

At the end of the first week, another little girl came right up to Sheba's cage. "Look, Mama! This kitty has bright blue eyes just like me! Can I keep her?"

Sheba pranced and purred. So hopeful. "Yes, please keep me, my heart is yours."

Blue Christmas

"See you next year, Honey," said Jesse. "Hug the kids for me. I wish I could watch them open their Christmas presents in the morning."

"I will," said Lauren. "I love you."

"It's a blue Christmas," said Jesse.

"Four more months of your deployment are unfathomable. Please come home safe and soon, Jesse."

Jesse shut off the video call and shoved down the depression that was eating him alive. He hoped he could white-knuckle it long enough to get home and discharged. He would worry about his health then, mental or otherwise. He was unraveling and didn't know how many more patrols he could go on without coming completely undone.

The next day, intense combat in close quarters left Jesse slumped against a wall, unconscious and in bad shape. His squad rushed him to the medivac helicopter. Most thought he would die.

If he were conscious, he would have thought the same.

Months later, Jesse woke up at Walter Reed Army Medical Center with both legs missing below the knee. He only had one functioning eye left. Mercifully, he had no memory of the battle, and no idea how long he'd been in a coma.

His last clear memory was of the video call with his wife on Christmas Eve.

Consciousness brought a new battlefield. Jesse had to relearn everything the injuries wiped out. The therapists told him it was great news that he still had half of his legs because he could be fitted with prosthetics. He would likely be able to walk and run.

Jesse didn't feel great about it. "And the eye?" he asked. "I suppose even a (half) blind man knows when the sun is shining."

His joke fell flat. They didn't have anything more to say.

Jesse was consumed with guilt for leaving his buddies in Afghanistan and for coming home to Lauren a different man.

He quickly got sick of the constant activity, noise, interruptions, poking, prodding, talking and fussing-over at the hospital. Jesse withdrew, stopped making eye-contact, stopped complying with myriad requests and suggestions. He stopped working hard in all the therapies ordered for him.

Jesse longed to be invisible from humanity and all its expectations. He couldn't even hide in slumber. Sleep was its own battle. It didn't bring peace, it brought violent nightmares.

After a nurse found Jesse on the floor thrashing and yelling, his unseeing eye wide open in terror, his medical team added a new component to his treatment plan: Animal-assisted therapy.

"I know the perfect dog for him," said one therapist. "Blue."

Blue was found locked in the bathroom of an abandoned house. He had no food or water, and was mere hours from death. He'd shredded the walls, cabinets and floor trying to get out and to get water. He'd shredded his paws and mouth in the process.

His ears had been cut short by a savage. He was covered in sores and scars and was missing a hind leg. The animal control officers knew it would be tough to get him adopted. The vet knew he had a long road ahead.

However, Hannah, an animal shelter volunteer, knew the compassionate depths of his heart the moment she looked into his eyes. She glimpsed Blue's future. And her own.

The first day Blue went to meet Jesse, he was enmeshed in a nightmare. He was soaked with sweat, yelling and swinging at an unseen, unreachable enemy.

Hannah tried to keep Blue in the doorway to Jesse's room. She was new at AAT work. She wanted to help the heroic soldiers at the hospital. But she also loved Blue and didn't want to risk getting him hurt.

Blue, built like a velvet-covered tank, with unmatched determination, yanked free of Hannah's grasp and scrambled across the slick tile floor to Jesse's side.

Blue gently placed his heavy head on Jesse's flailing hand. He pressed down, gentle and firm.

Jesse's body began to relax.

Blue calmly crept up onto Jesse's arm, then chest, and rested his big head on Jesse's shoulder. He placed his velvety-soft muzzle alongside his face.

Blue knew instinctively what all of the humans didn't.

Jesse needed the touch of Nature to heal.

Jesse took a deep breath for the first time in months and opened his eye. He was shocked to feel so calm. He was breathing normally. Then he felt the velvet on his face and the comforting, soothing pressure on his body.

It took a few deeply peaceful moments for him to question the source of his comfort.

Blue slowly raised his head and gave Jesse a tiny slurp on the forehead. Jesse connected with the kindest canine eyes.

Blue, the Rescued, became Blue, the Rescuer.

"Daddy, Daddy! When will Blue get here?" asked Kit and Kam in stereo, as twins do.

Christmas Eve was different, life was different, a year after that video chat. The house was decorated, the gifts wrapped and under the tree. Jesse was pretty sure that the twins would have Blue dancing in their heads that night instead of sugarplum fairies. Blue's visits were always the "Best. Days. Ever!" according to the twins.

Deep relief and gratitude permeated the festive air with relief that Jesse was home safe and gratitude that he was healing, working hard and making progress again.

Jesse was at last, glad to be alive.

Hope was restored. It all began with Blue's healing touch.

Jesse and Lauren snuggled on the love seat as the twins watched for Hannah and Blue to arrive.

"He's here! He's here!" chimed the twins. "Blue's car is here!"

"Blue drives now, huh?" teased Jesse.

"Noooooo, daddy! Dogs can't drive," said Kit.

"Blue is magic! He can drive if he wants to," argued Kam

"No arguing. Let's go help Hannah with Blue," said Lauren.

Before the twins could get to the bottom porch step, Blue was on the top one, his big pink tongue at the center of his wide, joyous smile.

"Bluuuue!" squealed the kids.

"Hello, Hannah,"said Jesse. He always found it difficult to talk to Hannah because he didn't know how to express his deep gratitude for her. He believed that her intuitively *knowing* his need for Blue was a gift from God.

Jesse didn't know how to express to her that she and Blue had saved his life. They had also saved the loves of his life - Lauren, Kit and Kam - from a grief they could never fully heal from.

Jesse wanted to live, deep down, all along. But the noise in his mind, and the depression caused by his brain injury, told him otherwise at many points during his recuperation. He was always amazed that those moments when he nearly gave in, were the moments when Hannah and Blue would arrive. Those visits gave him enough of a break from the destructive thoughts for him to hold on a little longer.

"I have some news for you," said Hannah.

The entire family stood still, listening, and worrying. They had all learned to be cautious, to not expect too much, for fear that happy, normal moments could reverse in less than a heartbeat and crush them. Like the devastating news they'd received on the previous Christmas day.

"Whoa! Why the long faces?" asked Hannah.

"Sorry, Hannah. We get a little too tense when we hear the word 'news'," replied Lauren.

"Oh geez! I apologize! I did not mean to scare you guys."

Blue looked up at Hannah with his warm brown eyes.

"It's great news," she said. "I talked with the organization that rescued Blue. We all thought that Blue would spend the rest of his life with me."

The twins noticed the change in her voice, and the puddles growing in her eyes that were about to spill over.

Before they could arrive at a different conclusion, Hannah quickly sniffed and wiped her tears. "Blue is coming to live with you guys!"

"Dad! Mom! Is it true?"

Jesse was unable to speak. He was barely able to breathe. He'd never imagined it to be an option. He knew how much Hannah loved him.

"But what about your therapy work with the other Veterans?" asked Lauren.

"Well, I'm sure they will miss Blue's visits. But nothing like Blue misses Jesse when we leave," Hannah replied. "And I have more great news! I have been keeping a little secret."

She had the family's full attention, Hannah was an open book. They couldn't imagine her keeping secrets.

"I adopted a puppy a few months ago. We have been training together so that he can help Veterans too."

"Where's the puppy? Where's the puppy?" asked the twins as they jumped up and down in unison.

"He's at home right now. I promise you will get to meet him soon," she said. "Today is all about Blue and your daddy."

Jesse was quietly crying, no longer able to contain all of the emotion in his heart. "Hannah, you don't have to do this. I know how much you love Blue and how much he loves you."

"He adores you, Jesse. Dogs need *their person.* And you, my friend, are Blue's."

Blue moved to Jesse, as though on cue, as though he understood every human word. He looked up at Jesse as he leaned into his body.

Jesse looked into those captivating, trusting eyes, and said, "Welcome home, Blue. What an incredible surprise. I hope you are as grateful as I am."

Blue gave Jesse a tiny lick on the hand, laid down, and let out a deep sigh.

Lauren remembered Jesse letting out a sigh like that the first night he was home and falling asleep in their own bed.

Lauren laid her head on Jesse's scarred chest and whispered, "This is the best Blue Christmas."

Homecoming of the Heart

"Bombs leveled the entire village, sir," reported Major Davis.

"Survivors?" asked Lieutenant Colonel Gillan.

"Unlikely, sir."

"Hurry, help me dig! Hear that? Quiet, everyone. I heard a whim-per!"

The soldiers put down their shovels and clawed at the dirt and rocks with their hands. At last, one tiny, dust-covered face peeked out.

"Look at that! How did he survive?" Major Davis ripped his glove off with his teeth and gently cleared the ash and mud from the speckled pup's nose and eyes.

The puppy shook his head, took a deep breath, and began to pant. He looked so relieved, so happy to be freed of the rubble.

Davis caught a t-shirt someone tossed to him, wrapped the little survivor up and carried the vulnerable pup to their barracks.

Major Davis soon developed a second shadow. The pup followed him everywhere.

Davis noticed the pup had a "good nose" and could detect the faintest scents. He trained him to sit quietly when he smelled the components of explosives.

The pup loved to "work" with his human; it felt more like play.

Davis became deeply attached to the fuzzy little miracle he named Haps. In the dreary war zone, Haps infused light, joy and a playful zest for life, which Davis desperately needed.

Each deployment became more difficult to bear. He left more of himself in the decimated jungle each time he returned home. He felt hollow, and utterly drained of almost all that made him who he was...until Haps arrived.

As he finished up his year-long deployment, Davis was torn to shreds inside. He wanted out of the war, out of the jungle. But he could not bear to leave without Haps.

When he was given orders to return home, he frantically searched for any way possible to take Haps with him. To no avail.

Major Davis made his fellow soldiers *promise* they would care for Haps, and love him like their own.

The difficult day came when he had no choice but to board the chopper without Haps. Major Davis left his heart in the jungle.

Without Haps, Davis had a tough time adjusting to civilian life. He was depressed, anxious, and endured horrible nightmares. His injuries were far beyond the visible and physical. He had very little will to live.

Haps wasn't himself either. He was still a good little soldier, working hard for those who cared for, and loved, him. But his heart wasn't in it. He missed his master.

Davis tried every avenue to bring Haps home to the USA. It was the only reason he got up most mornings. But as months dragged on with no Haps, Davis became despondent.

After yet another surgery, while still drowsy from anesthesia, Davis saw the blurry smile of a person next to his bed. Then the unmistakable furry, smiling face of Haps bouncing up and down next to the woman in uniform.

"Hello, Davis," she said. "I have orders to deliver this wiggle-butt to you. He is yours. Forever, sir."

Davis thought he must be hallucinating. But then he felt a familiar cold, wet sensation on his fingertips, followed by a generous K-9 kiss. "Haps! It's really you!"

Haps jumped up on the bed to give Davis a proper, full-body, wiggly greeting. The canine soldier was home and reporting for his forever duty!

"Thank you, Lord. Now my heart is truly home."

New Year

"Grab your leash, Boogie! Let's go!"

Boogie jumped off the couch, lifted his leash out of his toy basket and proudly delivered it to Wren.

"You are such a good boy! You still know all your tricks from working with your daddy, don't you?"

At the mention of his daddy, Boogie's tail slowed and lowered. He missed his handler and partner as much as Wren missed her husband. Two years before, they lost him to a bullet while he was on patrol.

K-9 Officer, Boogie, lost a leg that same night, and a piece of his huge Pitbull heart.

Wren was on duty that awful night in her own precinct. She could never put on her duty belt and badge following that shift.

Wren, and Boogie, never reported for duty again.

Walking together helped them heal. At first, Boogie could only hop a few steps, but he was determined, and soon, unstoppable. Some days Wren only walked for Boogie's sake, other days, Boogie walked for Wren.

"Big night in the city, Boogie, New Year's Eve," said Wren. She sent up a silent prayer for safety for all the first responders on duty. Despite the familiar "New Year's Knot" in her stomach, she tried to be upbeat for Boogie.

Boogie smiled his best Pittie smile and offered her a cheerful wag. It was how they'd survived the past two years.

Suddenly, Boogie jerked his leash out of Wren's hand and rushed ahead to the next building, barking frantically and digging at the front door.

Wren ran to catch up, looked through the glass door, and saw the soles of someone's work boots. And smoke.

A wind gust flung the door open.

Boogie lunged inside and started tugging the victim toward the door.

Terrified, Wren followed. The air was unbreathable. Wren grabbed Boogie's collar and rushed them both outside.

Boogie flopped on the sidewalk, tongue lolling with fatigue.

Wren coughed and gulped in fresh air as firemen rushed past them to pull the victim to safety.

"Do you need medical attention, ma'am?" asked a police officer.

"No. I think I'll be fine," she said.

"How about your little pup?"

Wren looked around to see what little dog he was talking about. Boogie was so many things, but small was not one of them. She checked Boogie over carefully. He assured her that he was fine with a happy wag.

"My *little* pup?" she asked the officer. Wren noticed that he had very kind eyes.

He laughed. "Your little tank is welcome to have a seat in my vehicle with us while you give your statement."

Wren gave all the details she could recall, then got out of the car and called Boogie to follow.

He gave her the look; his infamous side-eye.

Wren knew he was up to something mischievous.

Boogie laid down on the seat of the car, closed his eyes and held still. To anyone but her, he looked sound asleep.

Wren commanded Boogie to come to her, then begged and bribed him too.

Still, Boogie "slept."

"How about I give you both a ride home?" asked Officer Miller. "It's cold."

Wren relented and climbed back in the car. An awkward silence filled the space, except for the calm, measured breathing of Boogie in the back seat—nothing like his usual panting and huffing from excitement on car rides.

"Make a right turn in two blocks. My house is the third one on the left after the turn."

Officer Miller started to say something but it came out as a dry croak.

"I'm sorry, what did you say?"

"Um...this is a first for me. Please forgive me if I'm being too forward. And awkward. But would you like to have dinner together...sometime?" he asked.

She noticed his face turning red. The tension was palpable. Electric. Wren was blushing too.

Wren took a few deep breaths, knowing it was time to take the next step forward. She knew that holding on to her grief in its current form could not last forever. It was exhausting. Unsustainable. She was also afraid to risk her heart. But she knew her husband wouldn't want her to be alone for the rest of her life. He would want her to be happy again. *It's just dinner, Wren. Chill out,* she told herself.

"What do you think Boogie?" she asked.

Boogie wagged the tiniest tip of his tail.

"At a restaurant with a dog-friendly patio, of course," added Officer Miller.

Boogie's tail thumped the seat hard and fast.

Wren allowed herself to smile. "That sounds terrific."

New year, new beginning.

Boogie wagged his whole tail, with all his heart.

Hope to the Rescue: A Hapless Camel Saves Her Hero

Late summer meant the cattail plants stood tall in and around the ditches and ponds of the ranch. Lauren, crumpled in their stems, was invisible. Cold irrigation water swept by, mere inches from her face.

An afternoon thunderstorm billowed in with breathtaking pace and power. The air crackled with electricity and clouds hung heavy.

Lauren's grandpa had taught her to always watch the sky. Storms in the high-altitude meadows surrounding their ranch could turn deadly in an instant.

That wisdom couldn't help her now.

Lauren had been hurrying near the irrigation ditch to adjust the head-gate. She needed to do that and then get the livestock safely into the barn. She also wanted to be warm and dry in her cabin before the storm hit.

As she ran, tall, wet reeds seemed to reach for her legs, grasping and entangling them like a snare. She tripped on an unseen rock. Her head hit the ditch bank, and her mind dimmed to black.

Hope Ranch was a continual hive of activity. The days were long and money always ran short. Hungry bellies needed feed, and veterinarian bills came far too often.

Ranch life sounds like a dream to some. Most have no idea of the work and worry involved. True ranchers, however, will not trade their lifestyle. They take the highs and the heartbreaks - though never in stride. Life and death are ever-present. A celebrated birth in the night might be followed by the death of another sentient being by sunrise.

Lauren was a born rancher. The ranch nourished her in ways nothing else could. When she was only fifteen years old, Lauren knew where she would live her life, and that she would be laid to rest in the family cemetery overlooking the ranch.

She knew that 365 days each year would begin long before the sun crested the alpine ridge that sheltered the eastern pastures, and that her days would be far from done when the sun slipped behind the peaks to the west.

She knew she would inherit the cattle ranch, including its boom-and-bust financial cycles. She had no idea, however, that while she stared down her approaching thirtieth birthday, she would become an orphan. A drunk driver had stolen her parents and upended her world.

Within the first year of her parents' deaths, she sold off the herd, and opened up her heart and her land to animals who had no one to love them; a business move that neighboring ranchers scoffed at.

Lauren almost agreed. It didn't make complete sense to her either, but it felt right. Her mom had taught her to always trust her intuition.

Lauren had no idea her last day on earth might come so soon, or in the cold water of the ditch she tended every water-turn. As she slid closer to the water, the sun lowered in the western sky. The air chilled her skin. Her time was running out.

Hope was the first large animal Lauren rescued. On a trip into town, Lauren spotted the camel in the mall's parking lot. The poor camel didn't have enough muscle or fat on her. Her hide sagged from her bones. Her coat was ragged and dull.

Tied to a horse walker by a short rope, the poor camel was forced to give rides to rowdy children while a carnival worker took souvenir pictures of her in her helplessness.

Lauren stopped her rig and bought a ticket for a camel ride; it was her way of getting a closer look at the camel, and the men handling her. Standing in the blazing August heat, she offered more money than she could afford to the carnival worker.

Lauren wasn't going home without the camel. She knew it was a risky move, but in her rescue-mind, she had no choice. She was ushered into the office trailer of the boss.

"How much for the camel?"

"Not for sale."

"Maybe you misheard me. How much, right here, right now?"

The boss laughed and looked up at Lauren. "How much do you have?"

"I can alert the authorities...perhaps they need to shut you down for a few days to check your whole setup for whatever illegal activity might be going on...or...a thousand dollars."

He looked out the filthy window of his trailer at the camel. He knew her time on earth was short. He'd wondered where he'd bury a beast that size while out on the road.

"Deal."

The boss followed Lauren out to the horse walker. He waved his workers away as Lauren unhooked the camel.

Lauren looked into the gentle, exhausted eyes of her new companion, "You'll never suffer like that again. I promise."

She led her rescued camel to safety, and Hope Ranch was born.

At her new home, Hope loved to browse among the trees. They were the first she'd ever been allowed to nibble on. Since Hope's rescue from the carnival circuit - where she'd been overworked, plagued with boredom, starved for food, water, rest, and kindness - her lanky frame was beginning to fill out.

Gentle companionship, and room to gallop under clear blue skies, also made her more playful and content. She adored Lauren, her sweet and compassionate caretaker.

"Hope! Get back here!" yelled Jeb, the newest ranch hand.

In a cloud of dust, Hope had disappeared from the tree line. Her nostrils flared. She'd picked up the scent of Lauren in the air and galloped to the ditch bank. Her pools of ochre-colored eyes searched for Lauren - her neck stretched to see over the top of the cattails.

"Hope! Dang it, get back here!" Jeb yelled, swiveling his head to make sure Miss Lauren didn't hear him yelling at Hope. She'd told him over and over since his hire, her animals were to only be spoken to kindly and treated with a gentle hand. He thought Lauren was a fool to think of animals that way. He saw them as dull-eyed, unfeeling, inferior property.

But Lauren saw all animals, including those labeled as livestock, as equal beings, deserving of love and kindness. She'd seen cows with their newborn calves, their gentle eyes full of love as they licked, nudged, and nurtured them to their feet.

She had a special love for her camel, Hope. They seemed to communicate as equal beings.

Hope trailed Lauren around the ranch while Lauren talked to Hope about the day's plans, the things they needed to accomplish, and little things like the names of new ducklings. Hope was a good listener and dear friend.

Lauren was Hope's whole world.

Hope peered over the reeds, sniffing, searching for Lauren. She smelled like love to Hope. As she picked up the scent, she narrowed her focus, and soon spotted one of Lauren's boots. Hope bleated and bellowed. Her eyes were wide with panic.

Jeb jogged up behind her. "Don't you kick me or spit at me."

He smelled like anger and fear to Hope.

"Get away from that ditch and get back to the barn! That storm's coming!"

Hope remained.

Jeb waved his arms, stomped his feet, and flailed his hat around in the air, trying to spook her away from the ditch.

Hope was immovable. She knew Lauren needed help. Hope continued to bleat and bellow in panic.

Jeb swatted Hope on the rump.

She ignored the insult.

He pushed and shoved his body against her, trying to make her move.

She refused to even glance at him. Hope only had eyes, ears, and heart for Lauren. She bellowed louder.

Finally noticing Hope's intense focus, Jeb spotted Lauren's bandanna. He punched 911 into his cell phone. Fearing the worst, he waded into the freezing water of the ditch, but was unable to find Lauren's weak, thready pulse.

First responders pulled Lauren from the thick mud that held her legs captive. They rushed her to the ER, hoping they'd get there in time.

The day Lauren returned home from the hospital, she tearfully greeted her animal family - her cats, dogs, sheep, cattle, horses and donkeys - all adored rescues. Her heart overflowed with gratitude and love.

As she gently held and kissed Hope's soft muzzle, she whispered, "I'll never be able to repay your love for me."

Hope curved her long neck around Lauren, her world.

Acknowledgements

To my husband, Jeff, your steady love, kindness and humor make *every* day an enjoyable adventure. Your consistent support keeps this writing dream alive and energized. I love you *LOTS!* It is a miracle in my mind that we met, that our hearts magnetically found each other and lit the fire of love and friendship that we share. Life with you is better than I ever imagined life could be.

To my family. My love and gratitude for you runs deep. I would not be who I am were it not for you. The best in me is because of the love, kindness and empathy you instilled in my character. I appreciate each one of you so much.

To my mom, thank you for a wonderful childhood, for developing a loving, lasting, friendship between us, and for instilling a deep love of books, writing, paper, pens, stories and companion animals.

To my sister, for your enthusiastic support, for reading my rough, unedited, *wild* NaNoWriMo drafts, and for printing a copy for me that made my book feel tangible, and made future books feel realistic and *inevitable*.

To Dani, thank you for making me feel so seen, for reminding me to be proud of the accomplishment of this book, and the work and heart it took to write and publish it.

To my friends who also keep me dreaming by asking how the writing is going. Your lack of doubt creates *belief* in myself as a writer.

To Dixie. Thank you. Your encouragement and gentle nudges made this possible. You made my dreams *reality*. I'm forever grateful.

To my writing friends at A Writing Room (https://awritingroom.com/) this book would have never happened without you. I am grateful for each of you. Keep going! Write. Edit. Publish. Repeat. Repeat. Repeat. Your words matter. YOU matter. You contribute, daily, to my joy of being a writer.

To Anne Lamott, Claire Giovino, Sam Lamott, Carly Vair and Meredith Morckel, A Writing Room would not exist without you. My heart is filled with gratitude for your kindness and support. Your efforts heal and change the lives of writers every day, mine included.

To my fellow Silent Writing leaders: Dawn, Daylan, Jules, Janet, Bernadette, Beth, Catherine, Jennifer, Dee, Daniel, Mere, Barby, Tricia, Sharlene, Ray, Tony, Anu and Tammy: your endless inspiration, encouragement, and dedication to writing and to our colleagues in A Writing Room keep the flames of creativity burning bright. You are truly the glue, and catalysts, of our beloved Community.

To Karen Loucks Rinedollar, my Writing Partner and dear friend. A huge heartfelt thanks. Your infusions of enthusiasm and energy continually spark the drive in me to open up my mind, see the world with awe and wonder, to write, learn, experience, write some more, and to publish often. I feel fueled up and raring to write with each conversation we share. http://creatingbeautifulchaos.substack.com/

To Jennifer Newcomb, thank you for your excellent workshops in A Writing Room on how to succeed at self-publishing, your encouragement, and your generosity in helping me, and many of our friends, make it to the finish line. You taught us that this is all possible, that we don't have to wait for the approval of gatekeepers, and proved to us that we could overcome any hurdle. https://www.jennifernewcomb.com/

To Jenn Nienaber, for designing the gorgeous cover for WALKING *WITH* DOGS: A Memoir. Coming soon. You are an incredible, generous graphic artist, Writer-with-w-capital-W, and friend. https://www.paperandclouds.net/

To Jerrie Miller, for sharing an important, necessary story…even though it hurt your tender, beautiful heart to relive the experience. The telling of it will save lives. Thank you! Keep writing. The world needs your heart and empathy.

To Paula Lee, for your tremendous help with editing. Your keen eye, and kind heart, has made me a much better writer. Keep writing! The world needs your novel!

To our small, but *mighty*, writing group. Each week, you inspire, encourage and amaze me. Karen Loucks Rinedollar, Jenn Nienaber, Pamela Meyer, Connie Simmons, Liz Levin, Jennifer Newcomb, and Tammy Douglas: This book would have *never* been published without you, your encouragement, and the momentum we build together. Keep writing, taking on the world, demolishing what does not serve us, and empowering women writers. Your brilliant voices ring truth and hope into the universe.